The Gospels and Acts
In Simple Paraphrase
with helpful explanations
together with
Running Through
the Bible

The Gospels and Acts
In Simple Paraphrase
with helpful explanations
together with
Running Through the Bible
by
Chris Wright

ISBN: 978-0-9954549-5-8

Also an eBook ISBN: 978-0-9935005-9-6

For full list of books and updated information:
www.whitetreepublishing.com

Published by
White Tree Publishing
Bristol
UNITED KINGDOM
wtpbristol@gmail.com

Contents

Introduction

The first part of this book is a paraphrase of the Gospels and Acts. A paraphrase of the Bible is nothing new. For example, between 1517 and 1524 the scholar Erasmus wrote a paraphrase of the whole New Testament, with helpful explanations and comments. In 1873-74 Charles Foster published a much acclaimed paraphrase of major sections of the Bible, also with simple explanations of various events along the way. In 2002 Eugene Peterson published a paraphrase of the whole Bible called *The Message*. There have, of course, been others less well known.

Foster's paraphrase had the rather misleading title of *The Story of the Bible* which implied to some that it was the history of how we got our Bible. Although the work was generally well received, Charles Foster admitted in the introduction to a later printing to receiving some criticism for "changing the words of the Bible". Presumably this criticism was directed to his changing the words of the King James translation. Erasmus wrote his paraphrase in Latin, and in 1549 it was translated into English, well before the publication of the King James Bible, so that wasn't an issue.

For this book, Chris Wright has taken the chapter headings and episodes in the Gospels and Acts from Foster's original book of 1874. There was no point in reinventing the wheel, and Foster did a wonderful job in compiling his book which sold in hundreds of thousands, but which would now of course seem very dated in its wording and its complete lack of speech marks. The format of the original book is used here as a template for a completely new edition in today's English.

It is important to bear in mind that Jesus and His followers would have spoken the Aramaic language, although Hebrew was definitely known by Jesus, because He was able to discuss the Hebrew Scriptures with the scholars in the Temple in Jerusalem at the age of twelve. *Koine* Greek was a commonly used language that may have been spoken by Jesus some of the time. *Koine* Greek means simplified Greek, also known as New Testament Greek. The Gospel and Epistle authors wrote their accounts of Jesus in *koine* Greek. We know Jesus spoke Aramaic, at least some of the time, when in the Gospel of Mark He says to the girl He has brought back to life, *"Talitha, cumi"* which is Aramaic for "Young girl, get up." (*Cumi* is spelt differently in various Bible translations.) In the garden of Gethsemane Jesus calls God *Abba*, the word a child would have used when speaking to his father. And on the cross, as Jesus feels the full weight of our sins, we are told by Mark that He calls out in Aramaic, *"Eloi, Eloi, lama sabachthani"* which in English is, "My God, My God, why have You forsaken Me?"

Koine Greek was known by most people in Israel at that time, not just by scholars. Neither Aramaic nor *koine* Greek were the sort of formal wording lawyers use, but were what ordinary people spoke to each other. This paraphrase uses informal English, while trying not to change the message of the Bible in any way at all.

Foster makes it clear in a later edition that his work is *not* the Bible, but a retelling of it in his own wording. This, of course, is what preachers do every Sunday when expanding on a Scripture passage, for which they (hopefully!) receive thanks rather than criticism. Sunday school and Bible class teachers do the same when they're telling the

Bible story. Exactly the same thing is being done in the paraphrase in this book, which makes no claim to be an exact translation of the original Greek. Of course, there are often several ways to understand the exact meaning of every event or parable. Here we give the generally accepted ones, but not all readers will agree on every point. Bear in mind that this paraphrase is not a deep theological work, but a quick look through the Gospels and the Book of Acts. Deeper study will definitely be needed to get to grips with some of Jesus' teaching!

In the English Protestant Reformation in the sixteenth century, the English translation of the Bible (known as the Great Bible) was required by law to be placed in every church in the land. It was held by a chain to prevent it being borrowed or stolen. But this was not all. The law also required Erasmus's English paraphrase of the New Testament, with helpful comments, to be placed with the Bible. A paraphrase of the New Testament was seen as essential in the Reformation, when for the first time ordinary people were able to get easy access to an English Bible. In the paraphrase they found helpful explanations about what they were reading, presented in a simplified wording of Scripture.

The paraphrase in this book combines the four separate accounts of Jesus' birth, life, death and resurrection from the four Gospels into one continuous narrative. This causes some problems because the events and parables told by the different Gospel writers are not always in what we would call the right order. This is how people wrote at the time, but it can be confusing today. So in his book Foster tried to give the Gospel records in a reasonable but not necessarily fully accurate timeline. Erasmus didn't have this problem, as he gave each Gospel its own paraphrase! Our paraphrase doesn't always keep to Foster's timeline, and adds some teaching and events he omitted, such as John's introduction to his Gospel; Jesus offering to take our burdens; Jesus saying He is the Way, the Truth and the Life. And in Revelation, Jesus promising that if we open the door and let Him into our lives, He will come in. There are several others.

White Tree Publishing wants once again to make it clear, as Charles Foster did for his own book, that this is *not* a Bible translation, but a paraphrase using many different words. Because spoken words here are often a shortened combination of several verses, sometimes taken from different chapters or Gospels, they must *not* be used by themselves to prove a particular point, or to quote as Scripture. All readers are encouraged to pick up whatever translation of the Bible they prefer, and read the Gospels and Acts for themselves.

White Tree Publishing acknowledges that the complete Bible is the inspired Word of God, but for anyone unfamiliar with the New Testament, this paraphrase with comments makes a valuable contribution, and it will surely help those already familiar with the New Testament to gain some extra knowledge and understanding as they read it.

Not sure how the whole Bible fits together? Abraham and Moses? The Exodus and the Exile? Confused over kings and prophets? Old Testament, New Testament? We'll start at zero, and assume nothing.

In Part 2 of this book we're running quickly through the Bible, and we won't be travelling alone. There's a red cord running with us, starting in Genesis where we begin our journey, through to Revelation at the end.

The red cord binds the Bible together. It's God's rescue plan for the people He created, giving us a way out of the mess we've made of our lives through the free will He has given us. A friend of the author who had just finished reading the whole Old Testament for the first time, told him, "It was written with God's tears."

Indeed it was. The friend could have added, "The New Testament was written with blood — the blood of Jesus."

Running Through the Bible by Chris Wright is available separately in both paperback and eBook format, also published by White Tree Publishing:

The paperback ISBN is 978-0-9927642-6-5
The eBook ISBN is 978-0-9933941-3-3.

Translators and others involved in foreign mission work, please note: If you believe that this copyright book, or part of this book, would be useful if translated into another language, please contact White Tree Publishing:

wtpbristol@gmail.com

Permission will be free, and assistance in formatting and publishing your new translation as an eBook and/or a paperback may be available, also without charge.

About the Author

Chris Wright has three grownup children, and lives in the West Country of England where he is a home group leader with his local church. He is the author of many books, mostly for young readers.

Part 1

The New Testament

The Gospels and Acts
in Simple Paraphrase
with a Summary of
the Epistles and Revelation
by
Chris Wright

Part 1 contents

John 1; Matthew 2; Luke 1-2

Jesus is the Word, and the Word is God; the birth of John the Baptist and of Jesus; angels appear to the shepherds; wise men from the East come to Bethlehem; Herod kills the children there; Joseph flees to Egypt with Jesus and Mary; Jesus attends the Passover.

JOHN in the start of his Gospel says, "Before time began, there was the Word, and the Word was with God, and the Word was God."

(The Word is Jesus, who when He came to earth said He was the Word of God and the Light of the World. In Revelation the crucified and resurrected Jesus is described as "dressed in a robe dipped in blood, and He was called the Word of God.")

John goes on to say, "He was in the beginning with God. He created everything." (Paul writing to the church in Colossae says about Jesus, "For by Him all things were created, in heaven and on earth.")

Still writing about Jesus, John continues, "In Him was life, and the life was for the people of the world. The light shines in the darkness, and the darkness cannot defeat it." (Jesus said of Himself, "I am the Light of the World. Whoever follows Me will not walk in darkness, but will have the light of life.")

Just over two thousand years ago it was time for the promised Messiah, the long-expected Saviour, to come on earth. The Old Testament tells how God promised, when Adam and Eve first sinned in the Garden of Eden, that a Saviour would come. It also tells how the prophets who lived later told the Children of Israel He was coming. But before He came, they said someone would be sent to tell the people to get ready for Him by repenting of their sins. This was John the Baptist.

While Herod the Great was king in Judea there was a priest called Zacharias living in Jerusalem. He and his wife Elizabeth were both old, and the Bible says they led good lives and were careful to obey all God's commandments. But God had never given them a child.

As in Old Testament times, the priests were divided into different courses or companies, just as King David had divided them. There were twenty-four of these courses. Each priest took his turn in staying for a time at the Temple to attend to God's worship. The course of priests Zacharias belonged to was called the course of Abijah (or Abia).

Every morning in Jerusalem, before it was light, the priests at the Temple began work. Some of them went to the altar of burnt offering to clean it, taking away the ashes that had been left there from the previous day, and putting fresh wood on the fire which was never allowed to go out. Other priests went into the Temple to trim the lamps on the golden candlestick, called the menorah, and clean the golden altar of incense. Afterwards, one of the priests offered up a lamb on the altar of burnt offering, and another burned incense on the golden altar.

The lamb was offered up, and the incense was burned at nine o'clock in the morning (called the third hour), and again at three o'clock in the afternoon (called the ninth hour). The day started at sunrise, which was approximately 6.00 am. These special hours were called the hours of prayer. At these hours the people came up to the Temple to worship, and stood in the court praying, while the incense was burning in the holy place.

On a day when it was the duty of Zacharias to burn incense on the golden altar, he went into the holy place to burn it at the hour of prayer.

While Zacharias was in the Temple he saw an angel standing at the side of the golden altar, and he was afraid. But the angel said, "Don't be afraid, Zacharias, for God will give you and your wife, Elizabeth, a son. You are to call him John. He will not drink wine or any strong drink, and he will be filled with God's Holy Spirit from the time he's born. He will tell the Children of Israel about the Saviour who's coming, and teach many of them to be sorry for their sins and obey Him."

Zacharias said to the angel, "How can I possibly believe this, now we're both old?"

The angel said, "I am the angel Gabriel. I live in heaven and stand before God, to do whatever He tells me. He's sent me to tell you this good news. But because you've not believed it, you will be punished by being unable to speak, until the words I've spoken come true."

The people were waiting in the courts of the Temple for Zacharias to come out of the holy place. After a time they wondered what was keeping him so long. When he came out at last, they realised he was unable to speak, but he made them understand by signs that he'd seen a vision.

Six months later, God sent the angel Gabriel to Nazareth, a town in Galilee, to a virgin engaged to be married to a man descended from King David. Her name was Mary. She was a cousin of Elizabeth, the wife of Zacharias, and was also descended from David. When Mary saw the angel she was worried, because she had no idea why he was there.

Gabriel said, "Mary, don't be afraid. God has really blessed you. You will have a son, and you will call Him Jesus. He will be great, and will be called the Son of God. And God will make Him King over everyone who loves Him, for ever. God has also promised a son to your cousin Elizabeth."

Mary told the angel, "I'm the servant of the Lord. Let everything happen to me that you've said."

Then the angel left.

Mary hurried to the land of Judah, to the house of Zacharias and Elizabeth, to visit her cousin. She stayed with Elizabeth about three months. Afterwards she came back to her own home in Nazareth. Joseph, her fiancé, was a carpenter.

God gave Zacharias and Elizabeth the son He'd promised them. When the boy was eight days old, their neighbours and relations came together to dedicate him to God, and decide what his name should be. They wanted to call him Zacharias, after his father. But his mother, Elizabeth, said, "No, he is to be called John."

They said to her, "You don't have any relatives called John." And they made signs to his father, asking what he wanted the boy to be called.

Zacharias asked for a writing tablet, because he was still not able to speak, and wrote, *His name is John.* They were astounded, because Zacharias hadn't told them that the angel had given him this name in the Temple.

As soon as Zacharias had written the name, God gave him his speech back, and he was able to praise God out loud.

When the people heard what had happened, they said, "What sort of man will this boy grow up to be?"

As John grew, the Lord blessed him. When he became a man he lived in the desert, away from the rest of the people. One day it was time for him to preach to the Jews, and tell them about Jesus. This man, whom God had given to Zacharias and Elizabeth, was John the Baptist.

The Jews were servants to the Romans, and had to obey whatever the emperor of Rome commanded. One day the Emperor Augustus made a decree that all the Jews should have their names recorded and pay tax. He ordered everyone to go to the town or city where their father had lived, and Roman officers would register their names.

Mary was expecting the baby that the angel Gabriel had promised her. Perhaps she and Joseph were married by this time, or maybe they were still engaged. She and Joseph set out from Nazareth, where they were living, to Bethlehem where King David had lived, because they were descended from David.

When they reached Bethlehem there was no room for them at the inn, because it was already full of people coming to register. So they went into a stable to sleep. It was in the stable at Bethlehem that Jesus was born. Mary wrapped Him round with bands of cloth called swaddling clothes to keep Him warm, and put Him in a manger to sleep.

That night, there were some shepherds nearby, in the fields watching over their flocks. The angel of the Lord appeared to them, and a bright light shone all around them. The shepherds were frightened, but the angel said, "Don't be afraid, for I'm here to bring you good news which will give joy to everyone. Today, in Bethlehem, the city of David, a Saviour has been born. He is Christ the Lord. And this how you'll know Him: you'll find Him wrapped in swaddling clothes, lying in a manger."

When the angel had said this, suddenly a whole crowd of

angels appeared, praising God, saying, "Glory to God on high, and peace to all who love Him."

After the angels had returned to heaven, the shepherds said to each other, "Let's go to Bethlehem and see the things the angel told us about."

So they went quickly, and found Mary and Joseph, and the baby lying in a manger. Then they went out and told others what the angel had said to them. Everybody they told was amazed at what they said. Then the shepherds went back to their sheep, praising God for what they'd seen and heard.

When the baby was eight days old, His parents dedicated Him to God, and called His name Jesus, as the angel had told Mary, Although He was the Son of God, He came on the earth to be a man. He was to teach about God and set an example of how His followers should live, and later to die for the sins of everyone who comes to Him for forgiveness.

After this, Joseph and Mary took Jesus to Jerusalem and took Him to the Temple in Jerusalem, and offered up a sacrifice of turtle doves, or young pigeons, which was required by the Jewish law.

In Jerusalem, there was a man called Simeon. He was a good man who worshipped God, and was expecting Jesus to come into the world. He knew this because he'd studied what the prophets had written about the Messiah.

The Holy Spirit had promised Simeon that he wouldn't die until he'd seen Jesus. And now the Holy Spirit told Simeon to go to the Temple and wait. When Joseph and Mary brought Jesus in, Simeon knew who He was. So he took the baby up in his arms, and said, "Now, Lord, Your promise has come true, and I can die in peace because I've seen the Saviour."

An elderly widow called Anna lived near the Temple, and she was a prophetess. She used to go to the Temple every day and night to worship God. While Simeon was speaking, she came into the Temple where Jesus was, and thanked God because He had let her see Him. Then she went outside and told the people about Him, because many of them were waiting for the Saviour, the Messiah.

Some wise men came from a distant eastern country, who asked, "Where can we find the child who is born to be the king of the Jews? We've seen His star in the sky, and have come to worship Him."

God had sent a star that shone over the land where these wise men lived, so they could know that Jesus was born, so they had come to Jerusalem to find Him. But when they arrived in the city they couldn't find Jesus, and they asked the people where they could find Him.

King Herod heard what they said, and was worried because they were talking about a new king. He was afraid that the child might some day be made king over Judea, instead of himself, so he desperately wanted to know where Jesus was.

Herod gathered some scholars together who had studied the Scriptures, and asked them where the Christ (which means Messiah) would be born. They said, "In the city of Bethlehem, for this is what the prophet has said."

Then Herod called the wise men to see him, and sent them to Bethlehem. He said, "Go there and look carefully for the young child, and when you've found Him come and tell me, so I can worship Him too." He had no intention of worshipping Jesus, but wanted to kill Him so He wouldn't be a threat to his throne.

After Herod had spoken to them, the wise men left Jerusalem. As they went, the star they'd seen in their own land appeared to them again. When they saw the star they were excited, because it moved on in front of them and showed them the way until it seemed to stand over the house where the young child was now living. By this time Mary and Joseph had managed to find a proper house in Bethlehem to live in. The Bible doesn't say how much time had passed since the birth of Jesus in the stable, but it might have been a year or more.

Then the wise men went into the house and saw Jesus with Mary His mother, and they bowed down and worshipped Him.

In those days, people who came to visit kings brought presents with them. So the wise men brought presents for Jesus; things that were precious in the country where they lived. They gave Jesus gifts of gold, and frankincense and myrrh, which spoke of His Kingdom and foretold His death.

Then God spoke to the wise men in a dream, and told them not to go back to Herod. So they returned to their own country by another route.

When Herod learned that the wise men had disobeyed him, he was furious, and sent his servants to Bethlehem to kill all the children there who were two years old or younger, because he hoped that among them Jesus would be killed. But before Herod's servants came, the angel of the Lord told Joseph to take Jesus and Mary and flee to Egypt. So Joseph got up in the night and left for Egypt with his family.

Later, when Herod the Great had died, the angel spoke to Joseph again, and said, "Go back to the land of Israel, for the people are dead who tried to kill the young child."

Joseph did as the angel said, and he and Mary and Jesus returned and lived in the town of Nazareth where they had come from. In the rest of the New Testament, Jesus is often referred to as Jesus of Nazareth.

Every year, Joseph and Mary went from Nazareth to Jerusalem to keep the feast of the Passover. When Jesus was twelve years old, He went with them. This might have been His first visit since returning from Egypt. Perhaps Joseph was afraid that Herod's son, Archelaus, who was now ruler of Samaria, Judea, and Idumea, had inherited his late father's jealousy and would be searching for Jesus among the visitors to Jerusalem. But Archelaus had now died.

When the feast of the Passover was over, the family started for home. People who went to the Passover used to travel in large groups, with friends and neighbours going up to Jerusalem together. Some of them rode on mules and donkeys, but many of them walked all the way. It would have been with a group like this that Joseph and Mary started out to return to Nazareth. All day long they thought Jesus was with the people who travelled with them. When they looked for Him in the evening, they couldn't find Him, so they left the group they were travelling with and hurried back to Jerusalem.

It had taken them a whole day to reach the place where they missed Jesus, so it took them a day to get back to Jerusalem. It wasn't until the next day that they found Jesus in the Temple talking with some Jewish scholars, listening to what they said, and asking them questions.

All the scholars who heard Jesus were amazed at the things He said, for He was only twelve years old, and the scholars He talked with were men of great learning.

Jesus' mother said to Him, "My son, why have done this to us? Your father and I have been really worried, looking for You."

Jesus said, "Why have you been looking for Me? Didn't you know I had to be in My Father's house?"

He meant that God had sent Him to teach people, and explain the Scriptures to them, before He died on the cross for their sins. But Joseph and Mary didn't understand what He meant.

Then Jesus returned with His parents to their home in the town of Nazareth, where He lived with them, and obeyed what they said to Him. As He grew, God blessed Him, and those who were with Him loved Him.

Matthew 3, 4, 14; Mark 1, 6; Luke 3-4; John 1-4

John the Baptist preaches in the wilderness; he baptizes Jesus, who is then tempted by Satan; Jesus finds some disciples; He turns water into wine; drives the traders out of the temple; talks with Nicodemus; John is put to death; Jesus comes to Nazareth.

NEARLY twenty years go by before the Gospel writers tell anything more about Jesus and His cousin John the Baptist. During those years, Jesus grew to be a man, while still living in Nazareth. The people had no idea He was the Son of God, and John the Baptist had not yet told anyone about Him.

John was still living in the desert. His clothes were made from the coarse hair that grows on the back of camels, fastened round his waist by a leather belt. He ate food called locusts, which he found in the desert, and honey from the wild bees living in hollow trees.

One day, it was time for John to preach to the people. God told him to tell everyone to get ready for the Messiah by repenting of their sins. So John went into the quiet countryside by the river Jordan, and a huge crowd came to hear what he had to say. John told them that the Messiah, the Saviour who had been promised, was coming very soon.

John said the Jews mustn't think that their sins would be forgiven simply because they were descended from a good man like Abraham. They must obey God themselves.

Many who heard John preach repented of the things that were wrong in their lives, and were baptized by John in the river Jordan.

John told the people who came to hear him, "I'm baptizing you with water, but the Saviour who's coming after me is greater than I am. He will baptize you with the Holy Spirit."

John was telling the people that although he baptized them with water, he was unable to wash their sins away. Because Jesus was going to die for the sins of the world, only He could really wash away anyone's sins.

The next day John saw Jesus coming towards him, and he said, "Look, the Lamb of God. He takes away the sins of the world! This is the one I was talking about when I said, 'He's greater than I am.' I said this because He was living even before I was born.' But John didn't want to baptize Him. John said, "I need to be baptized by *You*. Have you really come to be baptized by *me*?"

John felt he needed to have his own sins washed away, but Jesus had no sins to be washed away. So why was Jesus baptized? It was because He came to earth to take peoples' sins away, so it was a picture of Jesus taking their sins in His body, and then washing them all away.

When John refused to baptize Jesus, Jesus told him that although he couldn't understand it now, it was still the right thing to do. Then John agreed, and went down with Jesus into the river Jordan, and baptized Him there.

While Jesus was coming out of the water, praying to God, the sky opened, and what looked like a dove came down from heaven and landed on Him. It was the Holy Spirit coming down in the form of a dove. At the same time God's voice spoke out of heaven, and said, "This is my Son, the one I love. I am so pleased with him."

<> <> <>

Jesus was now about thirty years old. After being baptized by John, He went into the desert and stayed there alone for forty days and nights. All that time He ate nothing, but fasted and prayed to God. It wasn't long before he was hungry.

The Old Testament book of Genesis tells how Satan tempted Eve in the Garden of Eden to disobey God, and so caused everyone to have sinful hearts. When Satan saw Jesus coming to give these new hearts, and make His followers clean in His sight, he knew he had to try and stop Him. So Satan went into the desert to tempt Jesus, as he had tempted Eve in the Garden. He said to Him, "If You're the Son of God, change these stones that are lying on the ground into bread. Then You can have food, because You're feeling hungry."

But Jesus knew why Satan had come, and He refused to obey Satan and make the stones into bread. He told Satan it was written in the Scriptures that people must be more careful to obey God, and do what's right, than to get something as important as bread when they're hungry.

Then Satan took Jesus to Jerusalem, onto a very high part of the Temple. Then Satan said to Him, "If You're the Son of God, throw Yourself down, for it's written in the Scriptures that the angels will hold You up as You're falling, in case You're injured on a rock."

But Jesus said it was also written in the Bible that people must not deliberately put themselves in danger to test whether God will save them from harm.

Finally, Satan took Jesus onto a high mountain, and showed Him all the kingdoms of the world at the same time, with their beautiful cities, their mighty armies, and their great riches. And Satan said, "I will give You all these if You kneel down and worship me."

Satan had come out into the desert specially to try and make Jesus do this. He didn't care if Jesus turned the stones into bread, or threw Himself down from the Temple. But Satan really wanted Jesus to obey him, and take him for His master. This was the reason why he promised to give Him all the kingdoms in the world (even though they were not his to give!) if He would only kneel down and worship him.

But Jesus told him, "Go away from Me, Satan, for the Scriptures say, 'You must worship the Lord your God, and serve only Him.'"

When Satan realised he was unable to make Jesus do as he said, he left Him. Then angels came to Jesus to help him.

Jesus returned to the river Jordan where John was preaching and baptizing people. When John saw Him coming, he said, "Look, the Lamb of God!"

He called Jesus the Lamb of God because He was to be offered up as a sacrifice on the cross, as lambs were offered up on the altar. There were two men who heard John say this, and they came to see Jesus. Jesus spoke to them, and took them to the place where He lived, and one of them, called Andrew, brought his brother Peter.

The next day two others, named Philip and Nathaniel, followed Him. All these men came to Jesus so He could teach them, and they became His disciples. A disciple is a person who learns something from someone who is wiser. All Christians are called to be disciples, but the New Testament talks about twelve special disciples who were chosen by Jesus, in addition to many other followers who are also called disciples, but were not part of the Twelve.

Jesus went into the town of Cana, which was in part of Galilee. There was a wedding taking place there, and Jesus went with his mother, Mary. Both Jesus and His disciples were invited to the wedding. Food was ready for them to eat, and wine for them to drink; but before the end of the feast, the wine was all gone.

When the guests wanted more, Mary said to Jesus, "There's no more wine." Then she said to the servants, "Do whatever He tells you to do."

There were six stone water pots in the house, which the Jews kept to hold water for ceremonial washing. Jesus said to the servants, "Fill the water pots with water."

They filled them to the brim.

Then Jesus said "Take out some of the water and carry it to the man in charge of the feast."

When they did this, the water was changed into wine. The man in charge of the feast had no idea Jesus had changed it into wine, although the servants knew. When he tasted the water that was now wine, he called the bridegroom to him and said, "Other people, when they give a feast, serve the good wine first. Then after people have had plenty, they bring out the poorer wine; but you've kept the best wine until now."

This was the first miracle Jesus did to show His power to the people. When His disciples saw it, they believed that He was the Son of God.

When it was nearly time for the feast of the Passover, Jesus went up to Jerusalem to keep it. When He came to the Temple, He found men who had brought oxen and sheep and doves into the court of the Gentiles, to sell for sacrifices. There were other men who had tables on which was Jewish money, which was called the half shekel. The Jews gave one of these half shekels to the priests every year to buy sacrifices, or whatever else was needed at the Temple.

The men at the tables were called money changers. They exchanged, or sold, the half shekels to those Jews who wanted to give them to the priests, and made a lot of money doing this. Jesus was not at all pleased to find men selling in the court of the Temple, and He made a whip from small cords, and chased them all out, as well as the sheep and the oxen.

He then threw the changers' money onto the ground, and tipped up their tables, and said to the men who sold doves, "Take them away. Don't make My Father's house a place for buying and selling!"

While Jesus was at the feast of the Passover, many believed in Him when they saw the miracles He did.

There was a man called Nicodemus, who was one of the Jewish rulers. He came to Jesus in the night, and said to Him, "Teacher, we know God has sent You to teach us what's right, for no one could do the miracles You do if God wasn't with him."

Jesus told Nicodemus that unless he was born again, that is, unless he had a new life from God, he couldn't be one of God's children.

The Old Testament says that while the Children of Israel were journeying through the desert they sinned against God, and poisonous snakes, or serpents, came into their camp and bit them. God told Moses to make a serpent out of brass and lift it up on a pole. When anyone who'd been bitten looked at that serpent, they were healed.

Jesus said to Nicodemus, "In the way Moses lifted up the serpent in the desert, so must I be lifted up." Jesus meant that He was to be lifted up on the cross, so anyone could look up to Him, and have their sins forgiven. "For," He said, "God loved everyone in the world so much, that He sent His only Son into the world to die, so anyone who looked up to Him in faith would not be punished, but would be forgiven and have a place in heaven."

Herod, who killed the little children in Bethlehem, was now dead, and his son, Herod Antipas, was ruler over the part of the land called Galilee. This Herod, like his father, was an evil man. He had married Herodias, his brother's wife, while his brother was still alive. When John the Baptist told Herod that this was wrong, the woman, whose name was Herodias, was angry and tried to persuade Herod to kill him. But Herod was afraid to kill John, because he had heard him preach and knew he was a holy man. Yet, to please Herodias, he took John and shut him up in prison.

While John the Baptist was in prison, Herod, on his birthday, made a great feast for the lords, high captains, and chief men of Galilee. Salome, the daughter of Herodias, came in and danced before them. Herod was pleased with her, and said, "Ask me for anything you want, and it will be given to you, even up to the half of my kingdom."

Salome went to her mother and said, "What shall I ask?" Her mother said, "Ask the king to order John the Baptist's head to be cut off, and brought to you here in a large dish."

So Salome hurried back to the king, saying, "I want you to give me the head of John the Baptist in a large dish."

Then Herod was very sorry, but because he had promised her, and because the men who were with him had heard him promise, he would not refuse. Immediately he sent one of his soldiers who cut off John's head in the prison. He brought it in a large dish to Salome, and she gave it to her mother. When John's disciples heard about it, they came and took John's dead body and placed it in a tomb, and went and told Jesus.

Jesus and His disciples went into a part of the land called Galilee. On the way there, they came to a small town in Samaria named Sychar. Just outside the town was a well, called Jacob's well, where the people came to get water. It was in the hot part of the day, and Jesus, being tired with His journey, sat down by the well on His own, while His disciples went into the town to buy food.

A woman came from the town carrying her pitcher to draw water. Now this woman didn't love God in her heart, and had done many things to displease Him. Jesus knew this, for He sees all our hearts and knows everything we have done. He asked the woman to give him a drink of water.

The woman said, "I'm surprised you're asking me for a drink! You're a Jew and I'm a Samaritan!" At that time, the Jews would have nothing to do with Samaritans.

Jesus said, "You don't know what God can give you. And you don't know who I am. If you knew, you would have asked Me, and I would have given you living water."

The woman said, "Sir, where will you get this living water? The well is deep, and you have nothing to get water with. Are you greater than our ancestor Jacob? He's the one who gave us this well. He drank from it, and his sons and all his animals drank from it too."

Jesus told her, "Everyone who drinks this water will get thirsty again, but anyone who drinks the water I give will never be thirsty again. The water I give people will be like a spring flowing inside them. It will bring them eternal life."

The woman said quickly, "Sir, give me this water. Then I will never be thirsty again and won't have to keep coming back here to get more water."

Then Jesus told her about the five husbands she once

had, and about the man she was living with now.

She was surprised, and said, "Sir, I see You are a prophet." She meant that Jesus was a person to whom God told things which other people didn't know. She also said to Jesus, "I know that the Messiah is coming into the world. When He comes He will explain everything to us."

Jesus said to her, "I, the One speaking to you — I am the Messiah."

Then the woman left her pitcher and hurried back to the town, and said to the people, "Come and see a man who told me all the things that ever I did. Do you think He is the Messiah?"

The people went out and saw Jesus, and begged Him to come into their town. So He stayed with them for three days, and they listened to the things He taught them. Then they said to the woman, "Now we believe in Him; not because you told us about Him, but because we have heard Him ourselves, and know that He is the Savoir who has come down from heaven."

From that time on, Jesus began to teach the people in the land of Israel, telling them that the Judgment day was coming, and that they must repent of their sins and put their trust in Him.

Jesus went back to the town of Cana where He'd changed water into wine. An official who lived in another city came to Jesus and begged Him to heal his small son who was seriously ill. The official said, "Sir, come quickly, before my child dies."

Jesus said to him, "Go home. Your son is now well."

The man believed what Jesus said, and hurried home. Before he reached there, his servants met him and said, "Your son is now well."

The nobleman asked what time it was when his son began to get better.

The servants said, "The fever left him yesterday, at the seventh hour [1:00 pm]."

The man knew it was at the same time when Jesus said to him, "Your son is now well." Then the official and all his family believed that Jesus was the Son of God.

The Jews offered up their sacrifices only at one place, the Temple in Jerusalem. But they had special houses in every city where they met together to worship when they didn't want to offer up sacrifices or go to Jerusalem. These houses were called synagogues. Every Sabbath day the Jews met in them to pray and read the Scriptures. Their Scriptures were the same as our Old Testament, because the New Testament was only written until after Jesus was crucified.

As the people didn't yet know how to print books, they used to copy the different books of the Scriptures with pen and ink onto rolls of animal skin called parchment. These rolls, or scrolls, were kept in the synagogue in a box or chest called the ark, because it was shaped like the Ark of the Covenant that used to stand in the most holy place in the Temple.

When the people met together in the synagogue on the Sabbath day, the ruler of the synagogue sometimes asked one of the men to read from the Scriptures, and speak to everyone there.

Jesus came to Nazareth where He'd been brought up, and went into the synagogue on the Sabbath day. He was handed a scroll on which was written the book of the prophet Isaiah. When He opened the roll, He read to everyone from the part where Isaiah told the Children of Israel about the Saviour who was coming into the world.

After He finished reading, Jesus closed the roll and sat down. Everyone was looking at Him. Then He told them that those words of the prophet Isaiah had come true, and He was the Saviour, the Son of God, whom Isaiah had written about.

When Jesus said this, the men in the synagogue were angry, because they refused to believe that someone brought up in Nazareth could be the promised Messiah, the Saviour. They caught hold of Him and took Him to the top of a steep hill close to the city, intending to throw Him down and kill Him. But Jesus, because He had the power of God, was able to get away from among them, and they were powerless to hurt Him.

Matthew 4-12; Mark 1-3; Luke 4-6; John 5

Jesus teaches the people by the side of the Sea of Galilee; calls Peter, Andrew, James, and John to follow Him; prays in the wilderness; preaches the Gospel; heals the leper and the paralyzed man; calls Matthew; heals the man with the withered hand; chooses His twelve apostles; preaches the Sermon on the Mount.

IN CAPERNAUM, a town on the north west side of the Sea of Galilee, a huge crowd of people came to hear Jesus. As He stood by the water, people pushed around Him. He saw two boats on the shore, but the fishermen were not in them but were washing their nets. Jesus got into one of the boats, which was Peter's, and asked him to push it out a little way from the shore. Then Jesus taught the people from the boat.

When He'd finished teaching them, Jesus said to Peter, and Andrew his brother, "Sail out further, and let down your nets."

Peter answered, "Master, we've been fishing all night and haven't caught anything. But because You say so, I'll let down the net."

When they did this, they caught such a huge number of fish that the net broke. Then they called to their partners who were in the other boat by the shore, and asked them to come and help. Together, they filled both boats with so many fish that they began to sink.

When Peter saw the miracle Jesus had done, he knelt

down and worshipped Him, saying, "I'm a sinful man, Lord." For he was amazed by how many fish they'd caught, and so were his partners, James and John.

Jesus did this miracle so these men could believe in Him and know that He was the Son of God. He'd chosen them to be His disciples, to go with Him and learn from Him wherever He went. So He said to them, "Come with Me."

Because Jesus had chosen them to be His disciples and they had been following Him for a little time, they finally left their boats and their nets and everything they had, to become full time followers, full time disciples.

In the morning, getting up before it was light, Jesus went out to a quiet place to pray to God. Although He was God's Son, He had come on the earth to be a man; and while He was on earth, He felt pain and hunger and sorrow like everyone does. So He went out into the desert where He would be alone, and prayed to God for help, as people do today.

After Jesus had gone, the people came to Peter's house to see Him. So Peter and the other disciples decided to look for Jesus, and when they found Him, they said, "Everyone's looking for You."

Jesus said, "I have to go and preach the gospel in other towns and villages, as well as here."

Then Jesus went through the whole area of Galilee, teaching in the synagogues and preaching the gospel to the people. Gospel means good news. What good news was it that Jesus preached? It was this: That He had come into the world to be punished for people's sins, in their place, instead of them. That means that if anyone tells Him they're sorry for the things they've done wrong, and come to Him for forgiveness, that person won't be punished at the Judgment day, but washed clean and live in heaven where they will be with Him for ever. Jesus said He would never turn anyone away.

A man with leprosy came to Jesus, and knelt down in front of Him, and said, "Lord, if You want to, You can make me clean."

Jesus was sorry for the man, and put out His hand and touched him. Then He said, "I do want to. Be clean."

Immediately the leprosy went from the man, and he was free from the disease. Jesus sent him away and told him to tell no one who it was who'd healed him, but to go to the priest at the Temple and offer up a sacrifice, as Moses had told people to do if they were cured of leprosy. But the man, as soon as Jesus had gone, told everyone what Jesus had done for him.

Jesus probably told the man to keep quiet, because so many people kept rushing to see Him that He wasn't able to carry on with His plans for travelling and preaching.

Some of the Jewish leaders were called scribes, and others were called Pharisees, and they both claimed to be very holy. They studied the Scriptures (our Old Testament) and explained them to the rest of the people: but they didn't live the way the Scriptures told them to live. They obeyed some of the commandments, and were careful not to do any work on the Sabbath day (Saturday), and made long prayers in the synagogues, and even at the corners of the streets. But they did this because they wanted other people to see them, and then praise them for doing it.

These men were hypocrites, that is, people who claimed to be good, while in their hearts they were wrong. So when Jesus came, telling them they must repent of their sins and obey God, they hated Him, and did all they could to keep the people from believing in Him and trusting Him.

One day Jesus went back to Capernaum, and when the people heard He was there they gathered together at the house where Jesus was, and He taught them there. The houses of the Jews were often square, and one storey high. The roofs were flat, with a wall, or railing, around them, so that people could walk there in safety. In the centre of some of the houses was a large square room called the court. Over this, the roof was left open, but in time of rain, or too much heat, an awning or covering of some kind was stretched across the opening. Perhaps Jesus had come into a house like this, or maybe it was one with a roof of wooden planks covered in plaster to keep the rain out.

Some men brought a man who was paralysed and unable to walk, and wanted Jesus to heal him. When they couldn't come in at the door, because of all the people standing outside, they went up to the roof, and taking off the covering let the man down on his mattress, into the room where Jesus was speaking.

When Jesus saw how much faith the men had, He said to the paralysed man, "Your sins are forgiven."

Some of the scribes and Pharisees who were there, said to each other, "Who is this man who claims He's able to forgive sins, as if He were God?"

Jesus knew what they were thinking, and said, "Why are you asking this? Isn't it as easy for Me to forgive this man's sins, as it is to cure him of his paralysis? But to show you I have power to forgive sins, I will make him well." Then Jesus said to the sick man, "Stand up on your feet, pick up your bed, and go home."

Immediately the man sat up, stood on his feet, picked up

his mattress and walked out of the door to the crowd waiting outside. The people who saw it were astonished, and said, "We've never seen anything like this done before."

The Jews had to pay taxes, or tribute money, to the Romans. There were men in each town who collected these taxes from the people. The Jews hated the tax collectors, not only because they took their money to pass on to the Romans, but also because most of them were unfair and cruel men, often taking more than was right. Even so, not all tax collectors did this. As Jesus passed by, He saw one of them, called Levi, sitting in the place where the people came to pay the tribute money. He was also known as Matthew.

Jesus said to Levi, "Follow Me."

Levi immediately got up, left everything and followed Jesus, and became one of Jesus' disciples.

At the time of a Jewish feast, Jesus travelled to Jerusalem. In the city, there was a pool of water by the Sheep Gate. In Aramaic it was called the Pool of Bethesda. Around the pool were five porches in which sat a large number of people who were ill, or blind, or lame. They waited there, because at certain times the water moved, as if someone had stirred or disturbed it. The people thought that whoever got into the water first, after it was disturbed, would be healed from whatever disease they had.

A man was there who'd been ill for thirty-eight years. Jesus saw him, and knowing how long he'd been ill, took pity on him. He said to the man, "Do you want to be made well?"

The man said, "I've no one to help me into the pool when the water is disturbed. So while I'm trying to get down to it, someone else gets there in front of me, and I'm too late."

Jesus said, "Stand up, pick up your mat and walk!"

Immediately the man was healed, and he took up the mat he lay on and started walking.

This healing took place on the Sabbath day. The Jewish leaders, who wanted to find fault with Jesus, said to the man, "Don't you know it's against the law to carry your bedding on the Sabbath."

The man said, "The man who cured me told me to pick my mat up and walk."

They asked, "Who told you?"

The man said it was Jesus. Then the Jews tried to kill Jesus, saying He'd broken the Sabbath day.

Jesus talked with them, and told them that the miracles He did showed that God had sent Him. Jesus said the prophets also had spoken about Him, though the Jews refused to believe in Him. Jesus said He was the Son of God, and had power to raise the dead, as only God had, and that the hour was coming when all who were in their graves would hear His voice, and come out at the last Judgment.

Jesus could see how hard life was for many of the people. He told them to come to Him with their burdens. "Come to Me," He said. "Come all of you who are tired from the heavy burden you're carrying, and I will give you rest."

He tells all His followers to accept His teaching. He tells them that if they come to Him, "You will be able to get some rest for your souls. The teaching I ask you to accept is easy, and the load I give you to carry is light." So if one of His followers feels they are carrying a heavy burden, Jesus tells them to come to Him – and His followers must be sure to leave that burden with Him, and not take it away to keep carrying it again!

<> <> <>

One Sabbath day, Jesus was walking with His disciples through the cornfields. Because they were hungry, they picked some of the ears, and rubbed out the grains with their hands and ate them. When the Pharisees saw them doing this, they found fault, and said the disciples were working on the Sabbath. So Jesus told them that He wasn't to be judged for what He did on that day, because He was the Lord, or Master, of the Sabbath.

On another Sabbath day Jesus went into the synagogue, and a man was there whose hand was so deformed he was unable to open it or stretch it out. The Pharisees watched Jesus, to see if He was going to heal the man on the Sabbath. If He did, they could accuse again Him of breaking the Sabbath.

Jesus knew what they were thinking, and said to them, "If one of you has a sheep that falls into a pit on the Sabbath day, wouldn't you get hold of it and pull it out? And if it's right to do something good to a sheep, how much more is it to do good to a person. So I'm telling you it's all right to do good on the Sabbath day."

Then Jesus said to the man, "Stretch out your hand."

The man stretched it out, and it was made well like the other.

Then the Pharisees were furious with Jesus, and went out of the synagogue and discussed with each other how to find a way to put Jesus to death. When Jesus knew what they were planning, He left that place with His disciples, and went to the Sea of Galilee.

Crowds of people came to see Jesus, from Jerusalem and Judea, and from countries far away when they heard about the wonderful things He was doing. People who were sick crowded around Him to be made well just by touching Him; and He healed them all.

After this, Jesus went out to a desert place on His own, and stayed there all night praying to God. When it was morning, He called all His disciples and chose twelve of them to be with Him and to go out to preach. He gave them power to do miracles, to heal people who were sick, and to cast out devils.

Jesus called these twelve "Apostles", which means Messengers. They were Peter, Andrew his brother, James and John his brother, Philip and Bartholomew, Thomas and Matthew the tax collector, James and Lebbeus whose surname was Thaddeus, and Simon and Judas Iscariot.

When He saw the crowds that followed Him, Jesus went onto a mountain. When He was sitting down, His disciples came to Him and He taught them there. He told them which people were truly blessed and happy. Matthew in his Gospel doesn't make it clear how many disciples were there, but it is likely there was a large group of Jesus' followers, not just the Twelve, and probably many other interested people joined them, because Jesus taught for several days. Jesus may have spoken sometimes to His disciples, and sometimes to the whole crowd.

Jesus said:

"There are great blessings for people who know they are spiritually in need: the kingdom of God belongs to them.

There are great blessings for people who are sad now: God will comfort them.

There are great blessings for people who are humble: they will be given the land God promised.

There are great blessings for people who want to do the right thing more than anything else: God will satisfy them fully.

There are great blessings for people who show mercy to others: they will be given mercy.

There are great blessings for people whose thoughts are pure: they will be with God.

There are great blessings for people who work to bring peace: God will call them his sons and daughters.

There are great blessings for people who are persecuted for doing what's right: God's kingdom belongs to them."

Jesus told His disciples they must let their light shine. He meant they mustn't be afraid to let others know they love and obey God. Instead of hiding this, they must let others see it. Then, perhaps by their example, other people might also be led to love and obey God. Jesus said if anyone does the things God commands, and teaches others to do them, that person will be called great in the kingdom of heaven. But if, like the scribes and Pharisees, they only teach those things without actually *doing* them, they cannot enter into the kingdom of heaven.

He said to the people, "Your teachers have told you that if you kill another person, you're in danger of being punished. But I tell you that even if you get angry with someone, you will be in danger of punishment."

Jesus told His disciples that whenever they went up to the Temple in Jerusalem to worship God, they must try to remember whether they had done wrong to anyone; whether they'd taken anything that belonged to someone, or had said what wasn't true about them; or in any other way done someone harm. And if they had, they must go and put it right with that person. For God wouldn't accept, or care for, their worship while there was some sin still in their hearts.

Jesus said His followers must be pure and good in everything they do and say, and mustn't even think an impure or bad thought. And if an impure *thought* offends God, how deeply will the impure spoken word or action displease Him!

Jesus also said that when others are unkind to His followers, and harm them, they mustn't do harm back to them. Instead, they must do good to them, and pray for them, and love them. Jesus explained that if they do that, they will be the children of God the Father in heaven. So they must try to be like Him, perfect in everything they think and do and say.

Jesus told His disciples to be careful, in case when they do what's right, they do it only so other people can see them doing it, and then praise them. He said this isn't the reason why His followers should do what's right, by wanting to be praised. They should do it because they want to please God. Jesus said when one of His followers gives anything to the poor, they mustn't go about telling everyone. When they pray to God, they must avoid praying in a place where others can see them, but must go into their own room and shut the door, so no one but God can see. Then God will answer their prayers.

Jesus told his disciples that when they fast, they mustn't look sad, as the hypocrites did on purpose to let others know they were fasting; but they must look as cheerful as they did at other times, so no one but their heavenly Father would know they were fasting. Then their heavenly Father would reward them.

Jesus said His followers mustn't want to be rich, and save up a great deal of money in this world, but must lay up their riches in heaven. He didn't mean that they could lay up actual money in heaven, because no one will need money there.

Then Jesus said to the people, "You can't obey God, and

Satan, too." He said this because if His followers obey God, they'll be doing what's right, but if they obey Satan they'll do what's wrong. So they can't obey both. Anyone who comes to Him for forgiveness and a new life must choose who to follow and obey.

Jesus told His disciples not to judge other people. He meant they must be careful how they find fault with others, and then criticise them, for maybe that they never did the thing they get blamed for; or even if they did it, they didn't mean any harm. Only God can tell that, and maybe He doesn't blame them. And how often His followers do the very things they blame others for doing. Jesus said His followers should first stop doing wrong themselves, rather than finding faults in others that are also faults in their own lives – because maybe their own faults are worse faults!

He told the people who were listening to Him, and He tells His followers today, that whatever good thing they want other people to do to them, they must do it to others. If a follower of Jesus wants to be treated kindly and fairly, they must treat others kindly and fairly too.

Jesus also said, "Go in at the narrow gate, for there's a wide gate and a wide way that leads to destruction." He meant that the good and the bad ways are like two gates in life, and it's for people to choose which one to go through. The good way starts at what is like a small and narrow gate, that no one can see until they look for it very carefully. The bad way is like a wide gate that stands open in front of everyone. Jesus said this wide gate leads down to hell, and many people go there. The narrow gate leads up to heaven and Jesus said there aren't many people who find it.

Not everyone, Jesus said, who calls Him Lord, or Teacher, will be taken to heaven, but only those who obey His Father in heaven. Many people will come to Him at the

Judgment Day, and say to Him "Lord, Lord," and will tell Him how hard they worked for Him, and taught other people about Him. But Jesus will tell them they were never truly His disciples. He'll send them away, with everyone else who have led their lives without Jesus.

Then Jesus spoke about two men who each built a house. One chose to build on a solid rock. When it was finished, a great storm blew up and crashed against it. But the rain couldn't move the rock, nor could the wind blow the building away. So the man's house built on the rock stood firm, and the storm did it no harm. The other man built his house in a place where there was nothing but sand, so it had no proper foundations. The storm also crashed against it. The rain washed the sand away from underneath the house, the wind blew against it, and the house fell down and was destroyed.

Then Jesus said that anyone who listened to His teaching, and did what He taught them, was like the wise man who built his house on the rock. But people who listened to His teaching and took no notice or refused to believe what He said, were like the foolish man who built his house on the sand. Jesus meant that those who obey what He teaches them, and trust Him for forgiveness in this life, will be kept safe for eternity, no matter what happens, because their lives are built on the solid foundation of faith in Jesus. But those who refuse to follow Him now, are building on sand, and will be lost.

Matthew 8-13; Mark 4-5; Luke 7-12

Jesus heals the Roman officer's servant; raises the widow's son; is anointed; is ministered to; meets a scribe who wants to follow Him; tells the parable of the rich fool; tells His disciples not to fear hardship; tells five parables — the sower, the weeds, the mustard seed, the pearl, and the fishermen; stills the storm, and heals the demon-possessed man.

IN CAPERNAUM there was a centurion, an important officer in the Roman army. He had a servant he cared for very much, who was seriously ill and about to die. When the centurion heard that Jesus was in the city, he sent some of the older Jewish leaders who were his friends, to ask Jesus to come and heal his servant.

The elders came to Jesus and said, "Although this man isn't a Jew, but a Roman, he loves us and he's been kind to us. He's even built us a synagogue with his own money."

So Jesus set out with them towards the centurion's house. But before He got there, the centurion sent some more of his friends with a message to Jesus. The message said the centurion hadn't come to speak with Jesus, because he thought he wasn't good enough. And now he sent a message to say he didn't think he was good enough for Jesus even to come into his house. But if Jesus would only say that his servant would get well, without going to the house, the centurion was sure his servant would get well.

"I have soldiers under me," the Roman centurion said,

"and I say to one of them, 'Go,' and he goes where I tell him. To another I say, 'Come,' and he comes. So, I know the disease which my servant has will obey You and go out of him — if You just give the order for it to go."

When Jesus heard this He was astonished, and said to the people with Him, "I've not found a single person, even among the Children of Israel (the Jews), who has as much faith in Me as this Roman has. I tell you, at the last day many of the people of other nations who have believed in Me will be taken up to heaven, while the Children of Israel, because they refuse to believe, will be shut out."

When the centurion's friends returned to his house, they found the servant was now well.

The next day Jesus went into a town called Nain. As He came near to the town gate, the people were carrying out a dead man, and were going to bury him. He was a young man, the only son of his mother who was a widow. Many of her friends were with her.

When Jesus saw her, He took pity on her, and said, "Don't cry." He went forward and touched the coffin in which the body lay, and the people who were carrying it stood still.

Then Jesus said. "Young man, I tell you to sit up."

The young man sat up and began to talk, and Jesus gave him to his mother. Everyone who saw it was afraid, but they praised God and said He had sent a great prophet among them – meaning Jesus.

The people in eastern countries always took their shoes or sandals off when they went into a house, and a servant would bring water for them to wash their feet. The people also used oil, or ointment, to put on their heads and on the men's beards, and sometimes over their whole bodies. This was called anointing. They did it because it made the skin smooth and soft. They also thought it kept diseases away, because the smell of the ointment was sweet and pleasant. Men considered it a kindness to have their heads anointed by the owner of the house they were visiting.

A Pharisee, called Simon, invited Jesus to his house for a meal. There was a woman in the town who had lived a bad life, and people called her a sinner. When she heard Jesus was there with Simon, she came into the house with an alabaster box of ointment and knelt at His feet. She was now sorry for her sins, and wanted to be forgiven and lead a new life. Coming to Jesus, she wept, and washed His feet with her tears, and wiped them with her hair. Then she kissed His feet and anointed them with the ointment.

Simon the Pharisee knew the woman had a bad reputation in the town, so he looked at Jesus and said to himself, "If this man has *really* come from God, He'd know what sort of a woman this is, and He'd tell her to go away." He thought this because the Pharisees believed themselves too holy to let sinners touch them.

But Jesus knew what was in Simon's heart, and He said, "Simon, I have something to say to you."

Simon said, "Teacher, tell me what it is."

Then Jesus said, "Two men owed another man some money. One owed him a huge amount, and the other owed him just a little. But because neither of the men had any money, the man freely forgave them both. Tell me, now, which of them will love that man more?"

Simon said, "I suppose the one who was forgiven the larger amount."

Jesus said, "You're right." Then He turned towards the woman, and said to Simon, "Do you see this woman? I came into your house, and you didn't give me any water to wash My feet; but she's washed My feet with her tears, and wiped them with her hair. You didn't give me a kiss of greeting, but this woman hasn't stopped kissing My feet ever since I came here. You didn't anoint my head with oil, but she's anointed My feet with ointment. So let me tell you that her sins, which are many, are forgiven because she loved Me so much. Those who've only been forgiven a little, only love a little." Then Jesus said to the woman, "Your sins are forgiven. Go to your home in peace."

After this, Jesus went through every town and village preaching the good news to the people, and His twelve disciples, who were also called apostles, were with Him. He was poor, for although He could have been rich, because everything in the world was His, He chose to be poor and to suffer for those He came to save, to rescue them from being punished for their sins. Because He was poor, some of the women He had healed, and out of whom He had cast evil spirits, gave Him the things He needed day by day. One of them was called Mary Magdalene, another Joanna, and another Susanna. The Gospels give the names of these three, but there were many others.

A scribe, a teacher of the Law of Moses, came to ask Jesus a question. He said, "Teacher, I want to stay with You and go with You wherever you go."

Jesus said, "The foxes have their own holes in the ground and the birds have their nests, but the Son of Man doesn't have anywhere to rest." Jesus meant that He was even poorer than the foxes and the birds, because they had homes of their own, but He had no special place to go when He was weary and wanted to lie down. The scribe then went away

The Son of Man was a title Jesus sometimes used to describe Himself. In the Old Testament book of Daniel, the Son of Man was a powerful figure from heaven, seen in a vision. He would establish an eternal Kingdom that would include everyone. Jesus used the name again when He was on trial for His life before the crucifixion, and the priests knew exactly who He was claiming to be – the Son of God.

Jesus told the people a parable. A parable is a story which has a meaning to it, and which helps people understand and remember something they've been told. Jesus told the people this parable so they would know how foolish it was for them to put their trust in money.

He said, "There was a rich man who had many fields and vineyards. When harvest time came he gathered in his crops, but there was already so much in his barns that they wouldn't hold anymore. So he said to himself, 'What can I do? I've no more room to store my harvest.' Then he thought, 'I know what I'll do. I'll pull down my barns and build bigger ones, and I'll store all my harvest in them, and I'll even be able to store my other possessions. When I've done that, I'll say to myself, 'Now I can eat and drink and be merry, for I have enough riches stored away to last me for many years.'"

Jesus continued with the parable. "When the rich man said this, God said to him, 'You foolish man, you're going to die tonight. Who's going to have the things you've saved up for yourself?'"

Then Jesus said it will be like that with people who care only to save up riches for themselves in this world, but don't care to please God. Death will come when they're not expecting it, and then they'll have to leave their riches behind for others, and go away to a world where nothing has been laid up for them.

Jesus told His disciples not to be worried because they were poor, even though they might need food to eat, and clothes to wear. "Think of the birds," He said. "They don't sow seeds in the fields, or reap grain and take it to a barn to store it up there. Yet they always have enough to eat, because God feeds them. God cares more for you than He does for the birds. Look at the flowers, how they grow. They don't work like people to make clothes for themselves, yet they are more beautiful, and have brighter colours on them, than Solomon when he was king over Israel. So if God gives such beautiful clothing to the flowers, which are of so little value that one day they're growing in the field, and the next day they're cut down and burned, He will be more careful to clothe you, even though now you're afraid to trust Him. So don't be anxious when you need things to eat and drink and wear, because your heavenly Father knows you need these things. But first, seek to obey Him and be His children, and then He will give all you all the things you need. So don't worry about tomorrow."

While Jesus walked by the shore of the Sea of Galilee, large crowds came to see Him, so He got into a boat and sat in it to teach them. His voice came clearly over the water, and no one could come too close as they stood on the shore to listen. Jesus told them this parable. "A farmer went into his field to sow his seed, and he scattered it by hand over the ground. Some of the seed fell on the path that ran along by the edge of the field, and the birds flew down and ate it.

"Some of the seed fell on stony places, where there was hardly any earth. It started to grow, but because there wasn't enough earth to make proper roots, in a few days it withered away. Some seed fell along the side of the field where thorns and weeds were growing, and the thorns choked it as it started to grow. But the rest of the seed fell on the good ground that had been ploughed and made ready for it. The rain fell on the seed and watered it, and the sun shone on it, and it sprang up and bore grain, in some places up to a hundred times as much as the farmer had planted."

When Jesus was alone, His disciples asked Him to explain this parable to them. Jesus said that the seed stood for the words He preached. Some of the people who heard Him didn't understand what He said, nor did they bother to find out. Then Satan came and made them think of other things, and took Jesus' words out of their hearts as quickly as the birds ate up the seed that fell on the path.

Jesus said some of the people who heard Him remembered His words and tried for a little time to follow Him. But it was only for a little time. As soon as they had trouble, or were made fun of by others for following Him, they stopped trying, and turned away from Him. This was the seed that fell on the stony ground and started to grow, but in a few days it died away because it had no proper roots.

Jesus said that some of the people who heard Him speaking were glad to hear what He said, but then they went away and paid more attention to their houses, their money, and their pleasures, than they did to the things He'd taught them. This was the seed that fell among thorns, and the thorns choked it as it started to grow. But there were some people who listened to everything Jesus taught, and remembered it in their hearts, and trusted Him as their Saviour. Jesus said this was the good seed that took root and grew well, and bore up to a hundred times as much corn as the farmer had planted.

<><><>

Jesus told them another parable, also about a man who sowed seed. While the farmer's servants were asleep, an enemy came and sowed weeds among the wheat, and then went away, and the servants knew nothing about it. When the time came for the wheat to start growing, the servants went out in the field to look at it, and there they saw weeds growing among the wheat. They hurried back to the owner of the field and said, "Surely you sowed good seed in your field. So why are weeds growing with the wheat?"

The owner told them, "An enemy has done this."

Then the servants asked, "Do you want us to go and pull up the weeds?"

He said, "No, in case while you're pulling up the weeds, you pull up the shoots of wheat with them. Let them grow together until harvest, and then I'll say to my reapers, 'First of all, collect the weeds and tie them in bundles to burn them. Then harvest the wheat and store it in my barn.'"

Jesus then explained this parable to His disciples. He said the field means the world, and the owner of the field is Jesus Himself. The good seed means the things He taught, and the wheat that grew up is like people who listen to His words and obey them. The enemy who sowed the bad seed means Satan, and the weeds in the field mean wicked men. In the way the owner of the field allowed the wheat and the weeds to grow together until the harvest, so Jesus said He will allow good and bad people to live together in the world until the Judgment day. Then He will send His angels to gather up the good and take them to heaven, but the bad will be thrown into the fire.

Jesus told a parable about a mustard seed, which is one of the smallest seeds the people knew. He said when someone plants it in the ground, it grows to be their largest herb, and the birds come and perch in its branches. So it is with someone's love for God. At first it seems very small, but if they are truly one of His children, their love will go on growing, until they love Him more than they love anyone else, and will try even harder to please Him in everything they do.

Jesus then told the people about a trader who was looking for pearls to buy. He went to everybody who had any pearls to sell, hoping to find some that would suit him. At last he found one that was larger and more beautiful than any he'd ever seen before. But its price was so high he didn't have enough money to buy it. So he went away and sold everything he had, so he could come back and buy that one precious pearl. And this, Jesus explained, is the way people feel who want their sins forgiven. They cannot be happy until they're willing to give up everything that seems more important than God, so they are then able to come to Him and ask Him to forgive their sins – and Jesus said He will forgive us.

Jesus spoke about some fishermen with a net. He said they take it out to sea in their boat and throw it into the water and drag it slowly to the shore. When they pull it out of the water, they find a huge number of fish in it. But there are all sorts of different kinds of fish. Some are good, so they put these into baskets to keep; and some are no good for eating, and they throw these away. Jesus told His disciples that it would be like this at the end of the world. Then, He told them again, the angels will come and separate the godly people from the evil, and throw the evil people away.

In the evening, after Jesus had finished teaching the people, He went with His disciples in a boat to sail over to the other side of the Sea of Galilee. As they were going, a great storm blew up, and the waves crashed into the boat, filling it with so much water that it was about to sink. But Jesus was fast asleep in the back of the boat, with His head on a pillow.

His disciples woke Him up and said, "Lord, save us, or we'll all be drowned!"

Jesus got up and spoke to the wind and the sea, and said, "Be quiet! Be still!"

Then the wind stopped blowing, and the sea became calm. Jesus asked His disciples, "Why were you afraid? Why did you have so little faith?"

And the disciples wondered even more about who Jesus was.

They sailed over to the other side of the Sea of Galilee to the land of the Gerasines. When Jesus got out of the boat, He saw a man who had an evil spirit. The man had ripped off his clothes and was so violent that no one could go near him. He had often been tied him up with chains to keep him at home, but he broke the chains and went and lived in the burial caves that had been hollowed out of the hillside, to be used as tombs. Every night and every day the man was wandering among the tombs, screaming, and cutting himself with sharp stones.

When he saw Jesus coming, he ran to Him and fell down at His feet, and said, "What do You want with me, Jesus, Son of God? I beg You, please don't punish me."

Near the hillside a herd of pigs was feeding, and the evil spirits that were in the man (for more than one had gone into him), begged Jesus, that if He commanded them to come out, He would let them go into the pigs.

Jesus said to them, "Go!"

When the evil spirits had come out of the man, they went into the herd of pigs. The whole herd of about two thousand pigs them ran down the steep hill into the sea and were drowned.

The men who were looking after the pigs fled to the town and told the people what they'd seen. Then everyone came out to meet Jesus. When they saw the man who earlier had been possessed by evil spirits, sitting down quietly, fully dressed, and recovered in his mind, they were afraid, and they asked Jesus to go away.

When Jesus got into the boat to leave, the man Jesus had delivered from the evil spirits begged to go with Him. But Jesus said, "Go home to your family and friends, and tell them what wonderful things the Lord has done for you."

So the man went, and started to tell everyone how he had been healed by Jesus.

Matthew 9-14; Mark 5-6; Luke 8-9; John 6

Jesus heals the woman who touches His coat; raises the ruler's daughter; heals two blind men and a man unable to speak; sends out His disciples to preach the good news; feeds the five thousand; walks on the water, and heals the sick.

ONE DAY Jesus went to Capernaum, and one of the rulers of the synagogue, called Jairus, came to Him. Kneeling down at Jesus' feet, Jairus pleaded with Him, "My little daughter is sick and going to die. Please come and lay Your hands on her, so she'll live."

Jesus went with the synagogue ruler, and so did His disciples. Many people followed and crowded round Him. Among them was a woman who had suffered for twelve years from a disease which no doctor could cure, even though she'd asked many doctors to help her and given them all the money she had. Yet instead of getting better, she grew worse. When she heard that Jesus was there, she said to herself, "If I can just touch His coat, I'll be made well."

So she came in the crowd behind Jesus, and touched His coat. As soon as she'd done it she knew her disease was cured.

Then Jesus, turning towards the people who followed Him, said, "Who touched Me?"

His disciples told Him, "You see the crowd of people

pushing all round You, and You ask 'Who *touched* Me?'"

But Jesus looked to see who had done this. When the woman realised Jesus knew it was her and that she couldn't hide, she came trembling, and falling down at His feet she told everyone why she'd touched Jesus and how in a moment she was made well.

Jesus said to her, "Daughter, don't be afraid. It's because you had faith in Me that you're healed."

While He was still speaking to the woman, Jairus received a message that said, "Your daughter is dead, so don't trouble the Master any further."

But Jesus said to Jairus, "Don't be afraid. Just have faith, and she'll live."

When they came to the ruler's house, Jesus saw the people weeping and wailing. He said to them, "Why are you weeping? The child isn't dead, she's sleeping."

Jesus meant that she would soon come back to life like someone waking up. But they wouldn't believe Him, and started laughing at Him. Then Jesus put them all out of the house, and took three of His disciples — Peter, James and John — and the father and the mother of the girl, and went into the room where she was lying.

He took her by the hand, and said, *"Talitha, cumi"* which is Aramaic for "Young girl, get up." And the girl, who was twelve years old, got up and walked around. Everyone who saw it was amazed, and Jesus told them to give the girl something to eat.

As Jesus left Jairus's house, two blind men followed Him and shouted after Him, "You son of David, have mercy on us." They called Him this because He was descended from King David, and this was seen by many a title for the Messiah.

Jesus said to the men, "Do you believe I'm able to make you well?"

They said, "Yes, Lord, we do."

Then Jesus touched their eyes, and immediately they could see. Jesus said to them, "Don't tell anyone what I've done to you."

But when they left Him, they told everyone how He had healed them.

Some people brought a man to Jesus who was unable to speak, because an evil spirit had entered him. Jesus cast out the evil spirit, and the man spoke. All the people were amazed, and said, "We've never seen anything like this done before in all Israel." But the Pharisees who hated Jesus, told the people He was only able to cast out devils because Satan, the prince of the devils, helped Him.

Jesus returned to Nazareth, where He'd been brought up. On the Sabbath day He went into the synagogue and taught the people. They were astonished at the things He said. "Where did this man get such great wisdom, and power to do such wonderful works?" they asked. "Isn't He the son of Joseph, the carpenter? Isn't His mother called Mary, and aren't His brothers called James, Joses, Judas and Simon? Surely all His sisters are still living here in Nazareth. So how is He able to do all these things?" And they wouldn't believe who He said He was.

But Jesus told them, "People everywhere give honour to a prophet, but in his home town or in his own home a prophet doesn't get any honour."

Because of this, Jesus did no miracles in Nazareth, except He put His hands on a few sick people and healed them.

Jesus called His twelve disciples to Him to send them out through all the land, to preach the good news. He told them not to go into the cities and towns where the Samaritans or the Gentiles lived, but to only go to the Children of Israel, the Jews. He told them this because the Children of Israel were God's chosen people, and the good news was to be preached to them first.

Before the disciples went, Jesus gave them power to do miracles, so everyone who saw them do those things might believe the good news they preached. He said to them, "Wherever you go among the people, I want you to heal their sick, make their lepers well, raise their dead, and tell them that the Christ, the Messiah, has come to save everyone who believes in Him. But don't expect them to treat you kindly for doing this. As they've treated Me, so they will treat you. They will take you before their courts to try you and then beat you, because you tell them about Me. But don't be afraid of them. They're only able to kill your bodies. Instead, fear God who is able to destroy both soul and body in hell."

Jesus told the disciples not to take any money or food with them for their journey. He said everything they needed would be given to them along the way, because they were working for Him.

He told them, "You know that two sparrows are sold for almost nothing. They're worth so little that people care nothing for them. Yet God takes cares of them. He feeds them, and not one of them dies without Him knowing it. So don't be afraid that God will forget you, for you're much more valuable than sparrows. God remembers the smallest thing about you, and even knows how many hairs there are on your head. And He'll remember the people who are kind to you, for when anyone is kind to you it will be the same as if they were kind to Me. Whoever gives you a cup of cold water because you're one of My disciples, that person will be rewarded for doing it."

When Jesus had finished instructing His twelve disciples, He sent them out in pairs to travel through the towns and villages, telling the people about Him and healing those who were sick. Afterwards they came back to Jesus and told Him about everything they'd done.

Jesus said, "Come with Me and we'll find some quiet place where you can rest for a while," for there were so many people coming and going that they had no time even to eat.

They got into a boat and sailed to a desolate place near Bethsaida on the north of the Sea of Galilee to be alone. But when the people heard about it, they followed on foot, walking round the lake and arriving at the place where Jesus was with His disciples.

In the evening, Jesus' disciples came to Him, and said, "This is an isolated place where there's nothing to eat, and it's late now. You need to send the people into the villages to buy food for themselves."

Jesus said, "There's no need for them to go away. Give them something to eat."

The disciples protested, "We can't afford to buy enough bread to feed all *these* people!"

Jesus asked, "How many loaves do you have? Go, and see."

When they checked, they said, "Five loaves and two small fish."

Jesus told His disciples to make everyone sit down in groups on the green grass. Then He took the five loaves and the two fish, and looked up to heaven and thanked God for them. He broke the bread into pieces and gave the pieces to His disciples. He also divided the fish among them. And the disciples gave the food to the crowd.

Jesus made those few loaves and fish increase as they were given to the people, so there was enough for everyone. When everyone had eaten, Jesus said, "Collect up what's left, so nothing is wasted."

The disciples gathered up twelve baskets full of food that were left over. About five thousand men had eaten, as well as the women and children.

The people, when they saw this great miracle which Jesus did, wanted to make Him their king, but He left them and went up on a mountain alone to pray. He sent the disciples away in a boat to go across the Sea of Galilee to Capernaum.

In the evening, the disciples were out on the middle of the lake. They had to row, because the wind was against them and their sails were useless. Jesus was alone on the shore. He could see them rowing, and the waves were rough and stormy. In the early hours of the morning He went out to them, walking on the water.

When they saw Him, they were terrified, and said, "It's a ghost!" And they shouted out in fear.

But Jesus said to them, "Don't be afraid. It's Me."

Then Peter called out from the boat, and said, "Lord, if it *is* You, tell me to come to You on the water."

Jesus said to Peter, "Come on."

Peter got out of the boat and walked on the water to go to Jesus. But when he heard the noise of the wind and saw the great waves dashing around him, he was afraid and began to sink, and he called out, "Lord, save me!"

Immediately, Jesus stretched out His hand and caught him, and said, "You have so little faith. Why did you doubt?"

When Jesus and Peter got into the boat, the wind stopped blowing; and soon the boat was at the shore where the disciples wanted to be. Then they said to Him, "You really *are* the Son of God."

As soon as they got out of the boat, the people recognized Jesus, and ran through all the nearby towns and villages and carried people who were sick to where Jesus was. And wherever Jesus went, into towns and villages, they put the people who were unwell in the streets, and they begged to be able to touch Him, even if it was only His clothing. And the people who touched Him were made completely well.

Matthew 15-18; Mark 7-9; Luke 9-17; John 6

Jesus teaches the people; casts out an evil spirit; heals the deaf, the blind, and those unable to speak; feeds four thousand people; foretells His death; is transfigured; provides money in the mouth of the fish; tells the Parable of the Unforgiving Servant; James and John want to destroy the Samaritans; ten lepers are healed.

JESUS returned to Capernaum and went into the synagogue and taught the people. They asked Him, "What can we do to please God?"

Jesus told them, "Believe that I am the Saviour whom God promised to send into the world."

But the Jews were expecting the Saviour, when He came, to be a great soldier who would set them free from the Romans and make them into a powerful kingdom, and rule over them like the kings of other nations. The word "Christ" is Greek for the Hebrew word "Messiah," which is why people talk about "the Christ," meaning "the Messiah."

So when Jesus came to earth, not as a wealthy man but as a poor man, telling them to repent of their sins and obey God's commandments, and promising to reward them not in this world but in heaven, they were angry with Him, and refused to believe He was the promised Messiah.

Then Jesus said to His twelve disciples, also called apostles, "Are you also going away and leave Me?"

Peter said, "Lord, if we leave You, who can we go to, to be

saved?"

Jesus said, "I've chosen you twelve to be My disciples, but one of you is My enemy." He meant Judas Iscariot, because Jesus knew Judas was going to betray and sell Him to the chief priests and elders of the Jews, so they could put Him to death. The chief priests were the top in the different courses of priests who served by turns at the Temple. There were twenty-four chief priests. Like the scribes and Pharisees, they did all they could to keep the people away from following Jesus.

Jesus went to the cities of Tyre and Sidon, north of Israel. The people in those cities weren't Jews, but Gentiles. A woman who lived there heard that Jesus was there, and she went to Him and begged Him to cast an evil spirit out of her daughter. At first, Jesus turned away, as if unwilling to hear her because she wasn't a Jew. But He did this only to test whether she truly believed in Him. Then she begged Him more intently, and fell at His feet and worshipped Him. She said, "Lord, help me!"

Jesus said, "Because you have faith in Me, your daughter is made well."

When the woman returned to her house she found the evil spirit gone, and her daughter resting on the bed.

Jesus returned to the land of Israel, by the Sea of Galilee. The people brought a man to Him who was deaf, and could hardly speak, and they asked Jesus to lay His hands on the man so he'd be healed. Jesus took the man away from the crowd who were watching and put His fingers into the deaf man's ears, and spit and touched his tongue. Then looking up to heaven, He said, "Be opened." Immediately the man was made well, and he could both hear and speak.

Many people came to Jesus, bringing those who were lame, and blind, and unable to speak, and laid them at His feet for Him to heal them. Jesus healed them all, and the people were amazed when they saw the lame walking, the speechless speaking, and the blind able to see. Then they thanked God for what had been done to them.

The crowds being so large, Jesus fed them again with only a few loaves and some small fish, for they had been with Him for three days, and had nothing to eat. He said to His disciples, "I feel sorry for them. If I send them away to their homes without food, be so tired they may faint along the way, for many of them have come a long distance."

He asked his disciples, "How many loaves do you have?"

They said, "Seven, and a few small fish."

Jesus told the people to sit on the ground. Then He took the seven loaves and the fish, and thanked God for them, and gave them to His disciples to hand out to the people. Everyone ate and had enough. Afterwards they took up the pieces of food that were left: seven baskets full. About four thousand people had eaten, and Jesus sent them on their way.

Jesus came to the town of Bethsaida, and they brought a blind man and begged Jesus to touch him. Jesus took the man by the hand and led him out of the town. When Jesus had spit on the man's eyes and put His hands on him, He asked if he could see. The blind man answered, "I see men, and they look like trees, walking."

Then Jesus put his hands again on the man's eyes, and made him look up, and he saw everything clearly.

As Jesus came with His disciples towards the city of Caesarea, He asked them, "Who do the people say I am?"

They said, "Some say that You're John the Baptist who's come back from the dead; some say You're the prophet Elijah; and others think You're the prophet Jeremiah who's come back to the earth again."

Then Jesus asked, "But who do you say I am?"

Peter answered, "You're the Christ (meaning the Messiah), the Son of God."

Peter was telling Jesus that the disciples believed Him to be the Saviour whom God had promised to send into the world, although there had been, and still would be, times when they had doubts.

The Jews expected the Messiah, when He came, to set them free from the Romans and make them into a kingdom, and reign over them like other earthly kings. Even the disciples who were with Jesus all the time, and believed He was the Messiah, thought He was going to set up a kingdom here on earth. Although they could see He was now a poor man, they probably didn't think He would stay like that, but would soon become rich and powerful, and would make them all great too.

Like the rest of the Jews, the disciples hadn't yet learned that Jesus had come to rule only in their hearts, and to have His kingdom there; and that instead of fighting battles for them and ruling over them as a king, He was going to die on the cross for their sins.

From this time on, Jesus began to tell His disciples what was going to happen to Him: that He must go to Jerusalem and there be cruelly treated by the chief priests, the scribes and the elders of the Jews; and He would be killed by them, but would rise from the dead on the third day.

When Peter heard this, he was disturbed, and said, "No, these things will *never* happen to You!"

But it was to go through these things that Jesus had

come into the world, and when Peter said they must not happen to Him, it seemed as if he wanted Jesus to live and set up an earthly kingdom rather than die to save the people from their sins. So Jesus wasn't pleased with Peter, and called him His enemy, because Peter didn't want Him to do the things that would please God, but the things that would please Peter himself.

Then Jesus said that if anyone wanted to be His disciple, they mustn't look to find their own pleasure, but must take up their cross every day and follow Him. Jesus meant that His disciples must follow His example and do what is right, no matter how hard and painful it might be.

Jesus asked, "What good would it do anyone to have everything they wanted in this world, for as long as they lived; if, after they died, they lost their own soul?"

Six days later, Jesus took Peter, James and John, three of His disciples, and went up on a mountain to pray. While Jesus prayed, His face was changed, and it shone bright like the sun, and His clothing glistened and was white as snow.

Suddenly two men were there with Jesus. They were the prophets Moses and Elijah, who had come back to this world to talk with Jesus about His being crucified at Jerusalem.

When the disciples knew it was Moses and Elijah, and they wanted to stay on the mountain with them, and not go down again. Peter said, "Master, it's good for us to be here. If You're willing, let us make three shelters: one for You, one for Moses, and one for Elijah."

While Peter was speaking, a bright cloud came and covered them, and God's voice spoke out of the cloud, "This is My beloved Son. Listen to Him."

When the disciples heard it, they knelt down with their faces to the ground, and were really scared. But Jesus came and touched them, and said, "Get up. Don't be afraid."

When they got up and looked around, Moses and Elijah had gone and they saw no one except Jesus. Jesus said, "Tell nobody about what you've seen, until I've risen from the dead."

In spite of all the teaching Jesus had given them about what lay ahead for Him, they didn't understand what He meant when He spoke about rising from the dead, and they asked each other what He could mean.

The next day, when they had come down from the mountain, many people were waiting to see Jesus. A man knelt in front of Him, and said, "Master, I beg You, look at my son. He's my only child, and an evil spirit has entered him. It often makes him fall into the fire and into the water, trying to kill him. I took him to Your disciples for them to heal him, but they couldn't do anything to help."

Jesus said, "Bring him to Me."

As they brought the man's son, the evil spirit threw him to the ground, and he rolled around and foamed at the mouth.

Jesus asked the young man's father, "How long ago did this first happen to him?"

The man said, "When he was a child."

Jesus said to the evil spirit, "I command you to come out of him, and never go back into him."

Then the spirit, shouting out loudly, shook the young man severely and came out of him, but left him weak, like someone dead, and many of the people thought he really was dead.

But Jesus took the young man by the hand and lifted him up, and he stood on his feet and was well.

Jesus and the disciples went into Capernaum. The Jews who lived in the different towns and villages in the area used to send money to the priests at the Temple in Jerusalem, to buy sacrifices. The men who collected this money in the town of Capernaum came to Peter and asked whether his Master would give them any money. Jesus knew what the men were asking, and when Peter came into the room where He was, Jesus said to him, "Go to the Sea of Galilee and cast a fishing line into the water, and take the first fish you catch. Open its mouth and you'll find a coin inside. Give that to the men, as payment for Me and for you."

Peter did as Jesus told him, found the coin, and gave it to the men.

Although Jesus had told the disciples plainly what was going to happen to Him, how He would be treated cruelly and put to death at Jerusalem, they still didn't really understand Him when He told them this. They still expected, whatever Jesus might have to suffer, that afterwards He would set up an earthly kingdom and become great, and then they would also become great.

While they were walking along the road one day, the disciples began to argue with each other about which of them would be greatest in the kingdom they thought Jesus was going to set up. Jesus knew what they were saying, and when they came to the house they were going to, He asked them, "What were you were arguing about among yourselves along the way?"

They were ashamed and didn't answer Him. Then Jesus called a small child and placed him in the middle of them, and told them that unless they put away their pride, and their desire to rule over each other, they couldn't belong to the kingdom He was going to set up. He told them the person who is humble like a little child, will be the greatest in His kingdom.

He said, "If your hand or your foot causes you to do wrong things, cut them off and throw them away."

He meant that if His disciples were committing any sin, which they loved so much that it seemed as hard to part with as it would be to lose a hand or a foot, they must stop committing it and put it away from them. Jesus said it would be better for them to part with that sin, and at the day of Judgment be taken up to heaven, than to keep on committing it and be cast into hell.

Jesus told His disciples that whenever they met together in any place to worship Him, though only two or three of them might be there, He would be with them. He meant that His Spirit would be with them, as it was after He had died and risen from the dead..

He said if one of them sinned against another, and afterwards confessed their fault, the person they had sinned against must forgive them. Peter asked how many times they should forgive, whether as often as the seven times the Pharisees said they had to. Jesus told him they must forgive one another not only seven times, but seventy times seven. He meant always.

Jesus told the people a parable. "There was a king who wanted to find out how much money his servants owed him. One servant was brought who owed the king a huge amount of money, as much as ten thousand talents. A talent was 6,000 denarii, and one denarius was a day's pay for a worker. So the amount the servant owed was 60,000,000 day's pay, or something like 200,000 years of work! Jesus was making the point that the debt, like our sins, was far too great for anyone to ever be able to pay.

But as he had nothing to pay with, the king ordered the man and his wife and children to be sold as slaves. The money they were sold for was to be paid to the king towards the debt. Then the servant fell on his knees in front of the king, and begged the king to have patience with him until he could earn the money, or get it from those who owed it to him, "Then," the servant said, "I will pay you everything."

The king, when he saw the man's distress, pitied him, and forgave the whole debt.

But that same servant went out and found one of his fellow-servants who owed him one hundred denarii, which was a few months' pay. He caught him by the throat, and said, "Pay me what you owe."

His fellow-servant fell down at his feet, and begged him, "Have patience with me, and I will pay you everything."

The first servant refused, and threw him into prison, to be kept there until he could pay the debt.

The king's other servants saw what he'd done, and they told the king about it. Then the king, when he'd called the first servant, said, "You wicked servant. I forgave you your whole debt because you asked me to. Shouldn't you have pitied your fellow-servant as I took pity on you?" The king was greatly offended, and sent the servant to be punished until he paid all he owed.

In this parable the king means God, and the servant who owed God the impossibly large amount means everybody, because everyone has sinned so often against Him. As the king punished that wicked servant because he wouldn't forgive his fellow-servant, so, Jesus says, God will punish everyone who doesn't forgive each other their sins.

As Jesus travelled towards Jerusalem, He sent some of His disciples on ahead to prepare a place where He could stop and rest. They came to a village of the Samaritans, but the men from that village refused to let Jesus stop there, because He was a Jew and was going to Jerusalem. They didn't want the Jews worshiping at the Temple, where they were not allowed to go.

That made the disciples James and John angry, and they asked Jesus if He wanted them to call down fire from heaven to destroy those men. But Jesus wasn't pleased with James and John for asking this. He told them, "I didn't come on the earth to destroy men's lives, but to save them."

As they went on to another village, ten men who were lepers came to meet Jesus. These men stayed with each other because they were all sick with the same dreadful disease, and weren't allowed to go near people who were well in case they infected them. So they didn't come near Jesus and His disciples, but stood some distance away, and called out, "Jesus, Teacher, have pity on us."

The Old Testament tells that Moses had commanded every leper who was healed, to go and show himself to the priest, so the priest could give him permission to live among the people again. When Jesus heard these poor men crying out, He said to them, "Go now and show yourselves to the priest."

As they went, they were healed.

One of them, when he could see he was healed, turned back and praised God loudly, and knelt at Jesus' feet, thanking Him. The man was a Samaritan.

Jesus said, "Weren't ten of you healed? Where are the other nine? Only this Samaritan comes back to thank God for what's been done to him."

Luke 10-11; John 7-11

Jesus teaches the Jews; answers the lawyer's question; tells the parable of the good Samaritan; visits Bethany; teaches His disciples the Lord's Prayer; chooses seventy disciples; heals a blind man; says He is the Good Shepherd; raises Lazarus from the dead.

JESUS went up to Jerusalem, and the Jews were there to hear Him in the Temple. He sat down and said to the people, "I am the Light of the World. Anyone who follows Me will never have to live in darkness, because they will have the light that gives life."

Then the Pharisees said to Jesus, "When You make claims about Yourself, You're the only one saying these things are true. So we can't accept what You say."

So Jesus told, "You're right, I am saying these things about Myself. But people can believe what I say, because I know where I came from. And I know where I'm going. But you don't know where I came from or where I'm going. I am only going to be here with you for a little while, and then I'm going back to My Father who sent Me. After I've gone, you'll look for Me but you won't find Me. You can't go where I'm going. You won't believe I am the Son of God, and therefore you'll die without having your sins forgiven. But if anyone believes and trusts in Me, that person will never die."

Jesus meant that someone's soul would never die, but the Jews thought He meant the body would never die. So they said to Him, "Abraham has died, and so have the prophets, and yet You say that if someone believes and trust in You they'll never *die*. Are You greater than Abraham and the prophets?"

Then Jesus told them that Abraham, when he was alive, believed in Him, and knew He was coming on the earth; and Abraham wanted to see the day when He came, and in his heart, and by faith, he did see it, though it was then a long way off. Jesus said it made Abraham glad.

The Jews retorted, "You're not even fifty years old, and you're saying you've seen *Abraham*?"

Jesus told them that He was living in heaven before Abraham was born. At this they were furious and took up stones to throw at Him, but He slipped away from them and they were unable to harm Him.

On another day while Jesus was teaching the people, an expert on the law stood up to ask Him questions. He said, "Teacher, what must I do to be saved?"

Jesus said, "What does God's law command you to do?"

The lawyer said it commanded him to love God with all his heart, and to love his neighbour as himself.

Jesus told him, "You've answered correctly. Do this, and you will be saved."

But the lawyer may have wanted to test Jesus, because he asked, "And who is my neighbour?"

Then Jesus told this parable. "A man was going from Jerusalem to Jericho, and as he went he was caught by robbers who stripped him of his clothing and wounded him. Then they went away, leaving him half dead by the side of the road. While the man lay on the ground too weak to get up, a priest came by."

The lawyer understood what Jesus was saying. Because this priest was a teacher of God's law, he might be expected to show kindness to the wounded man. But Jesus said that instead of this, the priest crossed over to the other side of the road and went by, pretending he didn't see him.

Jesus said that after the priest, a Levite came along. A Levite also was one of those who attended to God's worship at the Temple: yet when he looked at the wounded man, he hurried on as the priest had done, without offering to help.

After the priest and the Levite had gone, a Samaritan who was on his journey came to the place. The Jews hated the Samaritans, and would have nothing to do with them. So the lawyer wouldn't have been surprised if Jesus said that this Samaritan also refused to help the wounded Jew. But it wasn't so; for when the Samaritan saw the wounded man, he went to him and tied up his wounds, after pouring in oil and wine to clean the wounds and help them heal.

Jesus said the Samaritan lifted up the wounded man, and putting him on his own donkey, took him to an inn, and nursed him there. The next day when the Samaritan left, he gave two silver coins to the owner of the inn, and said, "Take care of him. If you need more money to spend for him after I've gone, I'll pay you next time I come this way."

After Jesus had told the parable, He said to the lawyer, "Which of these three men do you think was like a neighbour to the man who was caught by robbers?"

The lawyer said, "The one who showed kindness to the wounded man."

Then Jesus said to him, "Then go and do the same." That is, to everyone who needs your help, do as the Samaritan did.

In the way that Jesus taught the lawyer, He teaches that whoever does good to another person, is that person's true neighbour.

<> <> <>

Jesus came to a village called Bethany, which was a little way from Jerusalem, and a woman called Martha invited Him to her house. She had a sister called Mary who, when Jesus had come, sat at His feet to listen to what He taught about the way anyone has to follow to be saved, and taken to heaven.

Martha, because she had all the work to do, was upset with her sister, and she came to Jesus, and complained, "Lord, doesn't it bother You that Mary has left me to do all the work? Tell her to come and help me."

Jesus answered, "Martha, Martha, you are careful and worried about so many things, but only one thing is important. Mary has chosen that, and it will never be taken away from her."

Jesus meant that Mary had chosen to come close to Jesus and listen to Him, putting Him first in her life. When she came to die, being close to Jesus and knowing Him, would be the only thing that was important, and the only thing that cannot be taken away from His followers today.

One of Jesus' disciples asked Him to teach them how they should pray. Jesus said, "When you pray, say, 'Our Father in heaven, may Your Name always be kept holy, may Your kingdom come. May Your will be done on earth as it is in heaven. Give us this day our daily bread. And forgive us our sins, as we forgive people who sin against us. And lead us not into temptation, but deliver us from the evil one.'"

Sins are the wrong things people do that hurt and displease God.

Jesus was telling His disciples to ask God for those things they needed, and God would give them. Jesus said, "If one of your children asks you for bread, would you give him a stone? Or if he asks for a fish, would you give him a snake?

So if you, who are sinful men, know how to give good things to your children, how much more certain is it that your heavenly Father will give the Holy Spirit to those who ask Him."

Jesus said that God would give His followers the Holy Spirit, because that is the best gift He can give; for it is the Holy Spirit who comes into people's lives and changes them into new lives, and so makes them God's children.

Jesus chose seventy more disciples, besides His twelve. He sent them out in pairs, into every town and village He was planning to visit, to heal the sick and preach the good news to the people. The seventy went and did as Jesus told them to. Afterwards they returned to Him, really happy, because they'd been able to do miracles in His name. But Jesus told them not to celebrate because they had power to do miracles, but rather because their names were written down among those whose sins were forgiven, and who would one day be taken to heaven.

One day, as Jesus came from the Temple, He saw a man who'd been blind ever since he was born. Jesus spat on the ground, and making clay with the spittle, He put it on the eyes of the blind man, and said, "Go and wash in the pool of Siloam."

The blind man went to the pool and washed. When he came back, he could see. Then his neighbours and other people who'd known he was blind, said, "Isn't this the man who used to sit and beg?"

Some people said, "It is," although others said, "He only looks like him." But the man said, "I *am* that man."

So they asked him, "How were your eyes opened?"

He told them, "A man called Jesus made clay and put it

on my eyes, and said, 'Go to the pool of Siloam and wash.' So I went and washed, and now I can see."

They said, "Where is He now?"

He told them, "I don't know."

They brought the man who'd been blind to the Pharisees. It was the Sabbath day when Jesus made clay and opened the man's eyes. The Pharisees asked him how he'd been made well. He said, "He put clay on my eyes, and I washed and now I can see."

Then some of the Pharisees told him, "The man who cured you can't be someone who obeys God, because He did it on the Sabbath day."

When the Pharisees asked him what he thought of Jesus, the man said, "I think He's a prophet."

But the Jews wouldn't believe that the man had really been blind until they called his parents and asked them, "Is this your son who, you say, was born blind? So how is he now able to see?"

His parents answered, "We know this is our son, and he was born blind. But we can't tell how he's able to see now. He's old enough to speak for himself. Ask him."

The parents were afraid to say it was Jesus who cured their son, because the Jewish leaders had agreed together that if anyone said Jesus was the Messiah, the Saviour, they would not be allowed into the synagogue. This is why the parents said, "He's old enough to speak for himself. Ask him."

Then the Pharisees again called the man who'd been blind, and said to him, "You must thank *God* for curing you, not the man who put clay on your eyes, because we know *He's* a sinner."

The man said, "I don't know if He's a sinner or not, but I do know I used to be blind, but now I can see."

They said to him again, "What did He do to you? How did he open your eyes?"

The man said, "I've already told you, and you wouldn't listen. Why do you want to hear it again? Are you also going to become His disciples?"

Then they ill-treated him, and said, "You are *His* disciple, but *we* are Moses' disciples. We know that God sent Moses, but as for this Man we don't know who sent Him."

The man said, "Why, this is a strange thing, that you don't know who sent Him, and yet He's opened my eyes. Since the beginning of the world, no one has ever heard of a man giving sight to someone who was born blind. If God hadn't sent this man, He wouldn't have been able to cure my blindness."

Then the Pharisees were angry, and told him, "You were born a complete sinner, and you try to teach *us*!" And they told him not to come into the synagogue again.

Jesus heard what the Pharisees had done, and when He found the man, He said to him, "Do you believe the Son of God is who He says He is?"

The man answered, "Who is He, Lord, so I can believe in Him?"

Jesus said, "You're talking with Him now."

Then the man said, "Lord, I believe." And he worshipped Jesus.

Jesus said to His disciples, "I am the Good Shepherd, and I know My sheep." He meant He was like a shepherd to His followers, and they were like His flock of sheep. In that country the shepherds went in front of their flocks, and the sheep followed them. Every sheep had a name, and knew the shepherd's voice and came when he called it.

The shepherd stayed with his sheep at night, as well as

in the day, to keep them from being lost, and to guard them from wild animals. So Jesus is always with His disciples to guard them from Satan, and help them follow Him closely.

In Jerusalem one day, as Jesus walked in the Temple, in Solomon's porch, the Jews came around Him, and said, "If You *are* the Messiah, who the prophets said would come, tell us that you are, plainly."

Jesus said, "I've told you already, but you wouldn't believe, because you're not My sheep. My sheep listen to My voice and they follow Me, and I will give them eternal life. They will never be lost, neither will anyone take them away from Me. My Father gave them to Me, and no one can take them out of His hand. I and My Father are one."

Jesus meant that He was God; yet not God the Father, but God the Son — as good and as great as God the Father, and to be loved and worshipped as much.

Then the Jews took up stones to throw at Jesus because He said He was God, but He escaped from them and left Jerusalem, going beyond the river Jordan to the place where John had once been baptizing. Many people came to Jesus and many believed in Him and accepted Him there.

Mary and Martha, who lived in the town of Bethany, had a brother called Lazarus, and he was seriously ill. So his sisters sent word to Jesus to tell Him their brother was dying. Jesus loved Martha and her sister and Lazarus, but when He received their message He didn't go straight to them, but stayed two days longer in the place where He was.

Afterwards, He said to His disciples, "Let's go to Bethany, for our friend Lazarus is asleep and I'm going to wake him out of his sleep." Jesus meant that Lazarus was dead, and He was going to raise him up from the dead. But Jesus' disciples thought He meant Lazarus was taking a rest. Then

Jesus told them plainly, "Lazarus is dead."

Bethany was near Jerusalem, about two miles away, and many of the Jews had already gone there to be with Martha and Mary, and comfort them in their loss. As soon as Martha knew Jesus was coming, she went out to meet Him, but Mary stayed at home.

When Martha met Jesus, she said, "Lord, if You'd been here, my brother wouldn't have died. But I know that even now, whatever You ask from God, He will give it to You."

Jesus said, "Your brother will rise and be alive again."

Martha didn't understand what Jesus meant, and she said, "I know he'll rise again at the Judgment day."

Then Jesus told her, "I am the resurrection and the life. Anyone who believes in me will have life, even if they die. Do you believe this, Martha?"

She said, "Yes, Lord. I believe that you are the Messiah, the Son of God. You're the One the prophets said was coming into the world."

Then Martha went back to her home and called to Mary, "The Master's here, and He's asking for you."

As soon as Mary heard this, she got up quickly to go to Jesus, and when she saw Him she knelt down, and said, "Lord, if You'd been here, my brother wouldn't have died."

When Jesus saw her weeping and the Jews weeping with her, He was deeply moved, and said, "Where have you put him?"

They said, "Lord, come and see."

Jesus wept.

Then the Jews, when they saw Him weeping, said, "See how He loved him;" and some of them asked, "Couldn't this man, who opened the eyes of the blind, have saved Lazarus from dying?"

Jesus came to the grave. It was a cave, and a stone was

rolled across the mouth of it to seal it. Jesus said, "Take the stone away."

Martha, the sister of Lazarus, said, "Lord, by this time his body will be decayed, for he's been dead four days."

Jesus said, "Didn't I tell you that if you believed in Me, you would see how great God's power is?"

Then they took away the stone. The Jews, when they buried their dead, wrapped the body in linen and tied a napkin around the head. This is how they had buried Lazarus. After the stone was taken away from the mouth of the grave, Jesus called out loudly, "Lazarus, come out!"

Then Lazarus came out with his hands and feet bound in the grave clothes, and his face tied round with a napkin.

Jesus said to them, "Free him, and let him go."

Many of the Jews who'd come to visit Martha and Mary, when they saw this great miracle which Jesus did, believed and trusted in Him. But some of them went to the Pharisees and told them what they'd seen.

Then the Pharisees and chief priests got together, and said to each other, "What can we do about this man who works so many miracles? If we leave Him alone, all the people will believe in Him, and make Him their king; and then the Romans will be furious and come and take away our city and destroy our nation."

They discussed with each other about finding a way to get rid of Jesus by putting Him to death.

Matthew 19-20; Mark 10; Luke 13-18

Jesus heals a woman on the Sabbath; explains what is needed in a disciple; tells seven parables — the lost sheep, the great supper, the lost piece of silver, the prodigal son, the rich man and Lazarus, the unjust judge, and the Pharisee and tax collector; He blesses some small children.

JESUS was teaching in one of the synagogues on the Sabbath day. A woman was there who'd been bent over with a disease for eighteen years, and was unable to straighten herself up. When Jesus saw her He called her to Him, and said, "Woman, you are healed of your disease." Then He laid His hands on her, and immediately she stood up straight and started praising God.

The ruler of the synagogue was angry because Jesus healed her on the Sabbath day. He said to the people, "There are six days in which men ought to work. If anyone wants to be healed, they can come, but don't come on the Sabbath."

Jesus said to him, "You hypocrite. Every one of you, on the Sabbath, takes his ox or his donkey from the stable and leads it out to give it water. And if it's all right to do what's necessary for the ox or the donkey, isn't it right that this woman, who's been suffering for eighteen years, should be made well on the Sabbath day?"

When Jesus said this, His enemies were ashamed; but the people were pleased because of the miracles Jesus did.

<><><>

On another Sabbath day, Jesus went to the house of one of the chief Pharisees, and while there He told a parable about a man who made a great dinner. Jesus said that when everything had been set on the table, the man sent his servants to the people who were invited, saying, "Come on now, everything's ready."

But they all made excuses. The first said, "I've bought a piece of land and must go and see it. Please have me excused." Another said, "I've bought five yoke of oxen, and I'm going to try them out. Please have me excused." And another said, "I've married a wife, so I can't come."

The servant told his master what had happened. The master was angry, and said to his servant, "Go out quickly into the streets and bring the poor, the lame and the blind into my house."

The servant did as he was told. Then he went to his master, and said, "I've done what you asked me, and there's still room for more guests."

The master said, "Go out again. Go through the streets and country lanes and *make* the people come in, and then my house will be full. None of the people who were first invited will taste my dinner."

In this parable the man who gave the dinner means God; the meal itself means the good news of salvation as God's children. The servant means God's ministers who preach that gospel; and the people who were first invited and wouldn't come are the Jews, because the gospel was preached to them first, and most of them wouldn't believe it. The men who were brought into the dinner afterwards, are the people of other nations who have heard the gospel since that time, and obeyed it. And then the command to go out into the streets and country lanes and bring them in, means that not only the rich and the great, but also the poor and unloved, are invited to come and be saved.

Great crowds came to hear Jesus. He told them that although someone might come and listen to what He had to say, if that person didn't in their heart care more for Him than for anyone else in the whole world, that person couldn't be His disciple. And if someone didn't take up their cross, that is, not think of themselves, in order to do whatever is right, as Jesus Himself did, they couldn't be His disciple. In the way that someone carrying their cross to their execution couldn't change their mind and go back, so becoming a follower of Jesus means no turning back, although of course His followers are going to live with Jesus one day in heaven!

"Which of you," Jesus asked, "who intends to build a house or a tower, doesn't first sit down and work out how much it will cost, and find out whether he has enough money to build it? Otherwise, when he's built only a little way, he may have to stop, and everyone who sees it will make fun of him, and say, 'This man began to build but wasn't able to finish.' Or what king who's going to make war against another king, doesn't, consider how large an army his enemy has, before he sets out, in case his own army is too small to fight against it?"

Jesus was saying that any person who wanted to follow Him must think first about what he or she would have to do. For unless they're prepared to give up everything they have, if Jesus told them to do it, they couldn't be His disciple.

The tax collectors (sometimes called publicans), and other people who were called sinners, came near to hear Jesus. The scribes and Pharisees found fault with Jesus because of this, and said, "He keeps company with bad people, and eats with them."

So Jesus asked them, "Which of you, if you have a hundred sheep, if he loses one of them, doesn't leave the rest and go after that lost sheep until he finds it? And when he's found it, he puts it upon his shoulders and carries it home, rejoicing. And then he says to his neighbours and friends, 'Rejoice with me, for I've found my sheep that was lost.'

"Or what woman who has ten pieces of silver, if she loses one piece, doesn't light a candle and sweep the house and look carefully until she finds it. And when she's found it, she says to her friends and neighbours, 'Rejoice with me, for I've found the piece of silver that was lost.'

Jesus used these parables to teach the scribes and Pharisees that the tax collectors and sinners who came to hear Him were like the lost sheep and the lost piece of silver, because they had done so many wrong things. Yet He wouldn't send them away, but would look for them, and encourage them to come to Him, so He could teach them to repent. Jesus said that even the angels in heaven were glad whenever one of these sinful people repents and begins to serve God.

Jesus told another parable. "There was a man who had two sons. The younger son said to his father, 'Father, give me my share of the wealth that will be mine some day.' His father gave him his share, and a few days later, the younger son took everything he'd been given and went away to a distant country, and there wasted the lot among evil companions. When he'd spent everything, a great famine came to that country and he needed bread to eat. He hired himself to a man who sent him out into his fields to feed the pigs. And he would have been glad to have some of the food the pigs ate, but the man didn't give him any.

"After he'd suffered a while, he said to himself, 'In my

father's house, at home, the hired servants have plenty to eat, and more than they want, while I'm here starving. I'll get up and go to my father, and say, 'Father, I've sinned against God and done wrong to you, and I don't deserve to be your son. Let me come back to your house, and treat me like one of your hired servants.'

"So he left that country to go back to his father. As he went, while he was still a good way off, his father saw him and took pity on him, and ran out to meet him, and put his arms round him and kissed him.

"Then the son said, 'Father, I've sinned against God and done wrong to you, and don't deserve to be your son.'

"But his father said to the servants, 'Bring out the best robe and put it on him, and put a ring on his hand and shoes on his feet; and bring the best calf and kill it, and let's have a feast and celebrate; for this is my son who left me, and now he's come back again. He was lost, and is found.' And they began to celebrate.

"The elder son was out in the field, and when he came near the house he heard music and dancing. So he called one of the servants and asked him what it all meant. The servant said, 'Your brother's here, and your father has killed the best calf because he's returned safe and sound.'

"Then the elder son was angry and refused to go in. So his father came out to him and begged him to join in the festivities. But he said to his father, 'For a great many years I've served you, and I've never once disobeyed your instructions. But you never gave me a feast for my friends. Yet as soon as your son comes home, who's wasted your money in living badly, you've killed the best calf for him.'

"The father said, 'My son, I've always loved you, and everything I have is the same as though it were yours. Yet it's right that we should be glad and celebrate, for your brother left us, and now he's come back. He was lost, and now he's found.'"

In this parable Jesus taught the proud scribes and Pharisees, who blamed Him for preaching to sinners, that God loved those sinners and was willing to forgive them and take them for His children again — if they would only stop living bad lives and obey Him.

Jesus told another parable to people who loved to be rich, spending their time enjoying themselves without any thought of obeying God. He said, "There was a rich man who was dressed in the most beautiful clothes, and ate the very best of food every day. And there was a beggar called Lazarus who was ill, and covered with sores. Because he was poor, and had nothing to eat, his friends carried him and put him down every day at the rich man's gate, so he could get the crumbs and pieces of food that were left from the rich man's table. And even the dogs seemed to pity him, for they came and licked his sores.

"The beggar died, and was carried by the angels to heaven. He was no longer poor, and didn't have to beg for his food. He ate at the table, resting on Abraham's side. Then the rich man died, but his soul went where the wicked go. In hell, while he was being punished for his sins, he looked up and saw Abraham in the distance, and Lazarus was with him. So he called out, 'Father Abraham, have pity on me, and send Lazarus to dip the top of his finger in water, and come with it and cool my tongue; for I'm tormented in this flame.'

"But Abraham said to him, 'Remember, in your lifetime you had good things, but Lazarus bad things; but now he's comforted and you are tormented. Anyway, there's a great gulf between us which no one can pass. Those who would like to go from us to you cannot, and those who would like to come to us from you cannot come.'

"Then the rich man said, 'If Lazarus can't come to me, I beg you to send him to my father's house, for I have five brothers living there. He can tell them to repent and obey God, so that when they die they don't come to this dreadful place.'

"Abraham answered, 'They have the Scriptures to read. Let them learn to repent from them.'

"Then the rich man said, 'No, Father Abraham, but if someone from the dead goes and speaks to them, they definitely will repent.'

"Abraham answered, 'If they won't hear what God says to them in the Scriptures, they won't be persuaded to obey Him, even if someone rises from the dead.'"

Of course, Jesus did rise from the dead, but many people refused to follow Him and put their trust in Him as their Saviour, and many still refuse today.

Jesus told another parable when He wanted to teach His disciples to continue to pray, and not be discouraged, even though God didn't at first seem to answer their prayers. He said, "There was a bad judge who didn't fear God, and didn't bother to act fairly towards people. In the same city was a poor widow who kept coming to him, and asking him to give her justice against a man who was her enemy. For a long time the judge refused to listen to her, but later he said to himself, 'Even though I won't do it because I fear God, or care to act fairly towards people, I'll do what the woman asks, because she's wearing me out.'"

Jesus said, "Listen to what this judge said. And if the judge, who was a bad man, did what the widow asked, because she asked him so often, won't God, who is holy and who loves His children, give them what they pray for by day and by night, even though for a time He doesn't seem to hear them?"

Jesus told a parable to people who thought they were more holy than others. He said, "Two men went up to the Temple to pray. One of them was a Pharisee and the other a tax collector. The Pharisee chose a place where the people could see him praying. He stood there proudly and prayed like this. 'God, I thank You that I'm not like other men, who are unjust, and who take more than belongs to them. I thank You that I am not a sinner like this tax collector. I fast twice in the week. I give to the priests and Levites a tenth part of everything I get.'

"But the tax collector, who felt himself to be sinful and was sorry for it, stood where he hoped no one would notice him. Bowing his head he beat on his chest in great distress, he said, 'God, be merciful to me a sinner.'"

Then Jesus told those who listened to Him that this tax collector went back to his home forgiven, rather than the Pharisee. "Because," Jesus said, "everyone who's proud and thinks a lot of himself will be put down, but the person who's humble and confesses his sin, will be raised up higher."

Some people brought their children to Jesus so He could put His hands on them and bless them. His disciples wanted to send the children away, but Jesus wasn't at all pleased. He said, "Let the children come to Me, and don't send them away. God's kingdom belongs to people who are like this." Jesus meant that only people who trust Him and love Him — in the way that small children love good parents — can come into His kingdom and be God's children. Then He picked the children up in His arms, and put His hands on them and blessed them.

As Jesus and His many followers journeyed together, Jesus took His twelve disciples aside and told them they were going with Him to Jerusalem, and when they got there all those things would happen to Him which the prophets had spoken about. He would be made fun of, be beaten and spit on, and then crucified; but the third day He would rise again.

His disciples, because they still thought Jesus was going to set up an earthly kingdom, were unable to understand what He meant when He told them this. The more someone trusts Jesus, and lives to please God, the more He will open their minds to understand things that have been hidden to them.

Matthew 21-23; Mark 10-12; Luke 18-21; John 12

Jesus comes to Jericho; heals blind Bartimaeus and visits Zaccheus; enters Jerusalem riding on a donkey; heals the blind and lame; curses the barren fig tree; tells the parables of the vineyard and of the marriage feast; explains which is the greatest commandment; and speaks highly of the woman who gave two small coins.

WHEN Jesus and his disciples went to Jericho, a large number of people followed them. A blind man called Bartimaeus was sitting by the side of the road begging. Hearing the crowd coming, he asked what was happening. They told him Jesus of Nazareth was coming by. As soon as Bartimeus heard this, he started to call out loudly, "Jesus, Son of David, please help me!"

When the people heard him calling out, they told him to be quiet. But he called even louder, "Son of David, please help me!"

Jesus stopped and asked the man to come to Him. So they called Bartimaeus, and said to him, "Come on, get up. It's good news. He's calling for you."

Then Bartimaeus stood up and threw away his coat to get to Jesus quickly.

Jesus asked him, "What do you want Me to do for you?"

Bartimaeus said, "Lord, I want You to give me my sight."

Jesus said, "Because you have faith, you are made well."

Immediately Bartimaeus could see, and he followed

Jesus, praising God for the miracle that had been done to him.

There was a man living in Jericho called Zaccheus, who was a chief among the tax collectors, and he was very rich. As Jesus walked through the streets of the city, Zaccheus tried to see who it was, but he couldn't because of the crowd. He wasn't as tall as the rest of the people. So he ran ahead and climbed into a sycamore tree, because he knew Jesus would be going that way. When Jesus came to the place, He looked up and saw him, and said to him, "Zaccheus, be quick and come down, for I must stay at your house today."

Zaccheus came down quickly, and going with Jesus he welcomed Him into his house cheerfully.

The tax collectors, who took the people's money for the Romans, were often dishonest and cruel men. They were unfair to poor people, often taking from them more than it was right to take.

It is very likely that Zaccheus did cheat people before Jesus came to his house. But when Jesus came, Zaccheus believed that God had sent Him, and he listened to Jesus' teaching and trusted Him.

Then Zaccheus stood up in front of all the people who were there, and told Jesus that he would be dishonest no more. He would be kind to the poor, he said, and give them half of all the money he had. And if he found he'd taken anything that didn't belong to him, he would give back four times as much to the person he took it from.

When Jesus saw how Zaccheus repented of his sins and obeyed what He taught him, He told Zaccheus that all his sins were forgiven. Of course, the Jewish leaders found fault with Jesus for going to the house of a tax collector because, they said, He'd gone to stay with a man who was a sinner.

Then Jesus told them He'd come into the world specially to go among people who were called sinners, to teach them to repent, and save them from being punished for their sins.

It was springtime and the feast of the Passover was near, and many people went up to Jerusalem to keep the feast. They were looking to catch sight of Jesus, and as they stood in the courts of the Temple they said to each other, "What do you think? Will He come to the feast?" They asked this because the chief priests and the Pharisees had given an order that if anyone knew where Jesus was, he had to tell them.

Six days before the Passover, Jesus came to Bethany where Lazarus lived, the man He had earlier raised from the dead. The people knew Lazarus was there, and they came to Bethany not just to see Jesus, but also Lazarus. The chief priests were now looking for some way to kill Lazarus, because many of the Jews, after they'd seen Lazarus raised from the dead, believed in Jesus and followed Him.

Jesus left Bethany to go to Jerusalem. When He reached the Mount of Olives, He sent two of His disciples on ahead, telling them, "Go into the village and you'll find a young donkey tied up, on which no one has ever ridden. Untie it and bring it to Me. If anyone asks, 'Why are you doing this?' say, 'Because the Lord needs it,' and immediately that person will let you take the colt to Me."

The two disciples went and found the young donkey, as Jesus had said. As they were untying it, the owners asked, "Why are you untying the donkey?"

They said, "The Lord needs it."

Then they were allowed to take it. And they brought it to Jesus, and the disciples put their outer clothing on the donkey and Jesus sat on it.

As Jesus rode towards Jerusalem, a crowd of people took off their coats and spread them out in the road. Others cut down branches from the trees and placed them along the road, where Jesus could ride over them. They did this to honour Him, for this is what the people did when a king rode through their streets. And the crowds in front of Jesus and the crowds behind Him called out loudly, praising Him, and shouting, "Welcome! God bless the king who comes in the name of the Lord. Let there be peace in heaven and glory to God!"

Jesus knew that although they were praising Him now, not all of them loved Him in their hearts, soon some of them would be crying out for Him to be crucified.

The Jewish leaders were angry to hear what the people were shouting, and told Jesus to tell His followers to be quiet. But Jesus said that if the people welcoming Him were silent, the stones on the ground would cry out in welcome.

As Jesus came near Jerusalem, He looked on it and wept when He thought of the suffering that was coming. He said their enemies would bring an army, and make a camp around the city, and besiege it and destroy it.

When Jesus came to Jerusalem, He went up to the Temple. Here, blind and lame people were brought to Him, and He healed them. But when the chief priests and the scribes saw the miracles Jesus was doing, and heard children in the Temple praising Him and calling out, Hosanna (which means Welcome), they were not at all pleased.

In the evening Jesus went out of the city to Bethany, and slept there. In the morning, as He came back to Jerusalem, He was hungry. Seeing a fig tree on the way, He went to it to eat some of the buds, but found only leaves on the tree. When the fig leaves appear in the spring they are accompanied by a crop of small buds called *taqsh*. These *taqsh* are eaten by travellers and others when hungry. They drop off before the real fig is formed, but if the leaves appear without any of these small buds, there will be no figs that year — and this tree had no *taqsh*. Then Jesus said to the tree, "Let no more fruit grow on you ever."

The disciples heard what He said. The next day, as they passed by the fig tree again, they saw that the tree had dried up from the roots, and it was dead. Remembering the words Jesus had used, they said, "Look how quickly the fig tree has died!"

Jesus was showing that this fig tree was the sign of the unrepentant Jewish nation. They refused to recognize Jesus as the Messiah, and therefore it was impossible for them to bear fruit.

Then Jesus told another parable. He said, "There was a man who planted a vineyard, and put a fence round it, and dug a winepress to hold the juice of the grapes when they were ready to be made into wine. He also built a watchtower so the servants could guard the vineyard against wild animals and robbers. After everything was finished, he rented his vineyard to farmers who were to give him a share of the fruit. Then he went away to a distant country.

"When the time came for the fruit to be ripe, the landowner sent one of his servants to the tenant farmers so they could give him his share. But the farmers caught the servant and beat him, and sent him away without anything. So the owner of the vineyard sent another servant. The tenant farmers threw stones at this one and wounded him in the head, and sent him away badly injured. Afterwards the owner sent yet more servants, and they beat some of them and killed others.

"Then the owner of the vineyard, having one son whom he loved, sent him, and said, 'Surely they'll be afraid to harm my son.'

"But the tenant farmers, when they saw him, said, 'This is the son, who, when his father dies, will inherit the vineyard. Come on, let's kill him and take the vineyard for ourselves.' So they caught the son, and threw him out of the vineyard and killed him."

Then Jesus said to the people who were listening, "When the owner of the vineyard comes, what will he do to the tenant farmers?"

The people said, "He'll destroy those evil men, and rent out his vineyard to others who will give him his share of the fruit."

In this parable the owner of the vineyard means God, and the wicked tenant farmers stand for the Jews who rejected Him. Two thousand years before this, God had chosen the Jews to be His people, and had given them the land of Canaan. He had taught them His laws, and they'd promised to obey Him. When they didn't do this, God sent His prophets to warn and persuade them. But they persecuted those prophets and killed them. Then, at last, God sent His only Son, Jesus. And now they were going to kill Him too, as the tenants had killed the son of the vineyard owner.

When the chief priests and the Pharisees heard this parable, they knew Jesus had said it about them, and they were angry and wanted to kill Him immediately.

Jesus told another parable to the people. He said, "There was a king who made a marriage feast for his son. He sent out his servants, telling everyone who was invited to come, but they stayed away. Then the king sent to them again, and said, "My oxen, my fatted calves, and my sheep have been killed for my feast, and everything is ready. So come to the marriage.'

"But some of the invited guests turned away and wouldn't listen, and others attacked the servants and killed them. When the king heard about it he was angry, and sent his soldiers and destroyed those murderers and burned up their city. Then the king said to his servants, 'The wedding feast is ready, but those I invited are refusing to come. Go out into the streets and country lanes and tell everyone you meet to come to the marriage.'

"So the servants went out and gathered all the people they could find and brought them in.

"Now the king had made new and beautiful clothes for the wedding guests, and these were offered to everyone as they came into the house, and they were told to put them on. But when the king went into the room where the feast was held, he saw a man who was not dressed for the wedding. So he said to him, 'Friend, how did you come in here without wearing the wedding clothes?'

"The man was silent, for he'd refused to take the clothes when they were offered to him. Then the king, being angry, said to the servants, 'Tie his hands and his feet, and take him away and throw him into the dark dungeons where those people are kept who won't obey me.'"

In this parable the king who gave the feast means God, and the king's son for whom it was given, means Jesus. Those who were first invited to it and wouldn't come are the Jews, because they were the first people to be asked to accept Jesus, but they refused. The people who were brought into the feast afterwards are those from other countries who have believed in Him since that time. And the man without the wedding clothes made by the king means anyone who claims to believe, but in his heart does not. For God sees people's hearts, and nothing they can do will hide them from Him, not even for a moment.

In several places the Bible tells people to put on clothes of righteousness, and to clothe themselves with Christ. In other words, to take the new life that Jesus gives, and be made ready for the great feast that is to come in heaven..

Jesus spoke to the scribes and Pharisees and called them hypocrites, because they loved to sit in the main seats in the synagogues and make long prayers there, because they wanted the people to see them doing it, and praise them for being so holy. However, at the same time, they were unjust to other people and cruel to the poor, taking for their own what didn't belong to them. For these things, Jesus said, they would receive the greater punishment at the Judgment day.

Jesus was sitting in the Temple court where the chests were placed into which the people dropped the money they gave to buy sacrifices. Many of the people who were rich gave a lot of money. But a poor widow came who gave two tiny coins called mites. Then Jesus called His disciples and told them that the two coins the poor widow had put in meant more to God than all the money the rich people were giving. For the rich people, Jesus explained, had plenty left for themselves, because they gave from their wealth; but the poor widow now had nothing left for herself, because she gave everything she had, even the small amount of money she needed to live on.

Matthew 24-26; Mark 13-14; Luke 21-22; John 12

Jesus foretells the destruction of the Temple; tells the parables of the ten virgins, and of the talents; speaks of the Judgment day; goes to Bethany again, where Mary anoints His feet; Judas agrees to betray Jesus for thirty silver coins.

ALTHOUGH the Jews had seen Jesus do many miracles, they refused to believe He was the Christ (the Messiah), the promised Saviour, because their hearts were full of sin. Even so, many of their rulers believed in Jesus, but were afraid to admit it, in case the Pharisees stopped them going to the synagogue; for they cared more about what people thought of them than they did about pleasing God.

We've already seen that Herod the Great had repaired the Temple and built it up with huge stones of limestone and marble. One of the largest limestone blocks in the foundations is more than forty feet (13 metres) long and weighs five or six hundred tons (tonnes). There were buildings for the priests to live in, standing near the Temple. We have also read of the splendid porches, with marble pillars, which stood around the court of the Gentiles.

As Jesus was going away from the Temple, one of His disciples said to Him, "Look at the beautiful buildings."

Jesus said, "I tell you the truth, the day is coming when these buildings will all be smashed to the ground, so not one stone will be left standing on another."

Jesus told His disciples to be always ready for the Judgment day, because no one knows how soon that day will come. Then He told them a parable about ten virgins, or bridesmaids, who went out to meet the bridegroom. In that country, when a man was married, some of his friends, each one carrying a lamp, would to go out to meet him when they knew he was near.

The ten virgins in the parable were ready to go out and meet the bridegroom. They had lit their lamps, but because the bridegroom was delayed, they sat down to wait for him. Eventually they all fell asleep. Five of them were wise, and had brought spare oil with them, as well as the oil that was in their lamps. If their lamps went out they would have enough to fill them again. But five were foolish, and had brought no oil except what was in their lamps.

At midnight the people who were watching called out, "The bridegroom is coming! Go out and meet him!"

Then all the virgins got up quickly and trimmed their lamps. And the foolish ones said to the wise, "Give us some of your oil, because our lamps have gone out."

But the wise said, "We only have enough oil for ourselves, so go out and buy some."

While they were gone, the bridegroom came, and those that were ready went in with him to the marriage feast. And the door was closed. Afterwards the other virgins returned and said. "Lord, Lord, open the door for us." But he said, "I don't know you." And he refused to let them come in.

In this parable the bridegroom means Jesus coming back to the earth on the Judgment day. The ten virgins are those people who call themselves His disciples, and who expect to be ready to meet Him when He comes. The oil in the lamps means true faith and trust in His followers' hearts. His followers must be sure to have enough of this to keep their lamps burning, that is, to keep loving Jesus and obeying His commandments. If they don't, when He comes again they won't go with Him to heaven. Like the foolish virgins whose oil was all gone, they'll find the door shut, and will never be allowed to enter. Becoming a follower of Jesus is not something to do lightly, without serious thought. Jesus warns in several places that once someone start this new life in Him, they must not turn back or even stop going forward with Him.

Jesus told another parable. This one was about a man who took a journey into a far-off country. Before he went, he called his servants and gave them money called talents to use to earn more for him while he was gone. He gave five talents to one servant, to another servant he gave two talents, and to another servant he only gave one talent. He gave each servant as much as he thought his servants would know how to use. Then he left on his journey.

The servant who had five talents took them and traded with them, until he earned five talents more for his master. The servant who had two talents did the same, until he earned two more talents. But the servant with one talent, because he was lazy and had no love for his master, dug a hole in the ground and hid his master's money, to keep it hidden until he came back.

After a long time the master returned, he called his servants to give an account of what they'd done. So the servant who had the five talents, said, "Master, you gave me five talents. Look, I've earned five more talents." His master said, "Well done, you're a good and faithful servant. You've worked hard and been careful with what I gave you. I'm now giving you many more things. Come and live in my house and be happy with me there."

Then the servant who had the two talents, said, "Master, you gave me two talents. I've earned two more talents beside them." And the master said, "Well done, you're a good and faithful servant. You've worked hard and been careful with what I gave you. I will now give you many more things. Come and live in my house and be happy there."

Then the servant who had the one talent, said, "Master, I knew you to be a difficult man, reaping where you didn't sow, and gathering where you didn't scatter seed. I was afraid in case I lost your money, and be punished for it. So I hid it in the ground where no one could steal it from me. And now here it is. Take it, for it's yours."

The master said, "You're a disobedient and lazy servant. Even if I were a difficult man, reaping where I didn't sow, that was no reason to neglect your duty and be lazy while I was gone. You could have put the money in the bank where it would have earned interest. You're just making an excuse for your own laziness." Then the master said to his other servants, "Take the one talent from him, and give it to my servant who's earned five talents. For to every person who has earned something, I will give more; but from the person who has earned nothing, I'll take away even the small amount he has."

In this parable the master means Jesus, who has gone to heaven to stay for a time, although no one knows how long this will be. But He *is* coming back on the Judgment day. The servants are all of Jesus' followers He's left to work for Him in this world. The talents are whatever He's given them to work with. Some Christians have many talents, and some have few, but everyone has as many as they know how to use.

When Jesus comes again, He will reward those who have used their talents in working for Him, but He will punish those who have been lazy and not used them, or who have used their talents only for themselves.

Jesus told His disciples what would happen on the Judgment day. On that day, He said, He will come in His glory, and all the holy angels will be with Him. Then He'll sit on His throne, and the dead from all the countries in the world will rise up from their graves and stand before Him to be judged. And He'll separate the godly from the evil, in the way a shepherd separates his sheep from the goats. He'll put the sheep on His right hand and the goats on the left.

Then He'll say to those on His right, "Come, My Father's children, into the kingdom which has been prepared for you since the beginning of the world. For when I was hungry you gave Me food; when I was thirsty you gave Me something to drink; when I was poor and naked you gave Me clothes; when I was sick you came to visit Me; when I was in prison you came to Me and comforted Me."

Then the godly will say, "Lord, when did we see You hungry and feed You? Or thirsty and give You something to drink? When did we see You poor and naked, and give You clothes? Or sick, or in prison, and comfort You?"

Then Jesus will tell them, "Whenever you did these things to any poor and suffering person who loved Me on earth, it was the same as if you did it to Me."

Then He'll turn to the evil ones on His left hand, and say, "Get away from Me, into everlasting fire that was made ready for the devil and his evil spirits. For I was hungry and you gave Me no food; I was thirsty and you gave Me nothing to drink; I was naked and you gave Me no clothes; sick and in prison, and you never came to visit Me."

Then they'll say, "Lord, when did we see You hungry, or thirsty, or naked, or sick, or in prison, and didn't help You?"

And He'll tell them, "Because you didn't do it to any of the poor and the suffering people who follow Me, it was the same as if you didn't do it to Me." And these will go away to be punished for ever, but the godly people will go and enjoy eternal life.

When Jesus had finished telling all these things to His disciples, He explained that in two days time it would be the feast of the Passover, and then He would be betrayed to be crucified.

The chief priests and scribes who were anxious to arrest Jesus, met together at the house of the high priest to scheme how they could do this, and then put Him to death. "But," they said, "we can't do it on the feast day when all the people will be here together, in case they become angry and cause a disturbance."

Meanwhile, Jesus was in Bethany, the town where Mary and Martha and Lazarus lived, and they gave Him a meal. Martha waited on Him, but Lazarus was one of those who ate at the table. The Jews didn't sit upright on chairs at their meals, but reclined, or lay down on couches placed around the table instead of chairs. They reclined on these couches, leaning on their left arms and feeding themselves with their right hands, while their feet were stretched out, away from the table, on the couches behind them.

As Jesus was reclining in this way, Mary took a container of ointment, called spikenard, which was extremely expensive, and bending down at His feet she anointed them with it, and wiped them with her hair. Then the house was filled with the sweet smell of the ointment.

One of Jesus' disciples, Judas Iscariot, who afterwards betrayed Him, said, "Why wasn't this ointment sold for three hundred denarii (a year's wages), and the money given to the poor?" Judas said this, not because he cared for the poor, but because he was a thief, and carried the bag in which the money was kept.

Jesus said, "Judas, leave Mary alone. Why do you find fault with her? She's done something good for Me. You have the poor with you always, and you can help them whenever you want, but you won't always have Me."

Then Jesus said to His disciples that wherever His gospel was preached, what Mary had done to Him would be told over the whole world, to remind people of her.

Then Judas Iscariot went to the chief priests, and said, "What will you give me if I take you to the place where Jesus is, so you can take Him alive?"

They promised to give him thirty silver coins, the amount a worker would earn in a month. From that moment on, Judas tried to find Jesus alone, so he could betray Him to them.

Matthew 26; Mark 14; Luke 22; John 13-18

Jesus and His twelve disciples eat the Passover; the disciples quarrel as to which of them will be the greatest; Jesus washes their feet; eats the Lord's Supper with them; goes with them to Gethsemane; prays in the garden; and is betrayed by Judas.

IT WAS the day when the Jews prepared for the feast of the Passover. To do this, each family or family group took a lamb to the Temple and killed it as a sacrifice. Then the priest burned its fat on the altar, and the people took the rest of the lamb to their homes to roast in the fire, and the families ate it in the night. Exodus chapter 12 explains how the first feast of the Passover was eaten in the night, when the Israelites were getting ready to leave Egypt where they'd been slaves. Care had to be taken not to break any of the bones, either during the cooking or during the eating.

Jesus and His disciples were going to keep this feast together, and the disciples asked Him where they should go to prepare for it. He said, "Go to Jerusalem and there you'll meet a man carrying a pitcher of water. Follow him into the house where he's going, and say to the man who lives there, 'The Master wants you to show us the room where He'll come to eat the feast of the Passover with His disciples.' The man will show you a large upstairs room that's already furnished. Prepare for the feast there."

The disciples did as Jesus told them, and the man

showed them the room and they prepared for the Passover there.

In the evening Jesus came to the upstairs room with His twelve disciples and reclined with them at the table. He said, "I have longed to eat this Passover with you before I die. I will no longer eat part of the lamb that's been sacrificed, until I've been sacrificed for the sins of the people."

The disciples didn't understand Him when He spoke of being sacrificed for the people. They still thought He was going to set up an earthly kingdom, and that the time for Him to do this was now near.

They began to quarrel among themselves again about which of them would be the greatest in that kingdom. Then Jesus told them that among the people of this world, those who were great ruled over the rest. "But," He said, "it won't be so with you. For whoever of you wants to be the greatest, let him be the most humble, and the one who wants to be in charge, let him be the servant of everyone."

Then Jesus asked them which was greater. Was it the person who ate at the table, or the servant who waited on him? Jesus said, "I am here with you as a servant."

To show what He meant, He got up from the table and took off his outer clothing. Then He took a towel and wrapped it around His waist. He poured some water into a basin, and began to wash the disciples' feet and wipe them with the towel which was around His waist. Then He came to Peter.

Peter didn't want Jesus to wash his feet, as though Jesus was his servant, and he said, "Lord, are You going to wash *my* feet?"

Jesus said, "You don't understand why I'm doing it now, but you'll understand later."

Peter said, "You will *never* wash my feet."

Jesus told him, "If I don't wash you, you cannot be one of My disciples."

Then Peter said, "Lord, don't wash just my feet, but my hands and my head as well."

Jesus said, "My followers are already clean and only need to wash their feet. And you are clean, though not all of you." He knew Judas was going to betray Him, and that was why He said not all of you.

After Jesus had washed the disciples' feet, and put on his outer clothing which He had put to one side, He returned to the table. He said to them, "Do you understand what I've just done? You call Me Lord and Teacher, and you're right, for that is what I am. So if I, your Lord and Teacher, have washed your feet, you ought to wash each other's feet, for I've given you an example of how to serve each other."

As they ate of the Passover, Jesus said, "I tell you the truth, one of you who is eating with Me will betray Me."

Then the disciples were sad and upset, and they looked at each other wondering who it could be. One of the disciples who Jesus loved was leaning on Him at the meal. The disciple was John. Peter signalled to him to ask Jesus who this was, so John said to Jesus, "Lord, who is it?"

Jesus said, "It's the one I will give a piece of bread to when I've dipped it in the dish." When Jesus had dipped the bread He gave it to Judas Iscariot. After that, Satan went into Judas. Then Jesus said to him, "What you're going to do, do quickly."

No one at the table knew what Jesus meant when He said this. Some of them thought, because Judas carried the bag in which the money was kept, that Jesus was telling him to go to buy things they needed, or else he was to give something to the poor. Then Judas left the house where Jesus and the disciples were. And it was night.

When Judas had gone, Jesus said to His remaining eleven disciples, "I will be with you only for a little while. Before I leave you, I'm giving you a new commandment. It is that you love each other. In the way I've loved you, so must you love each other. In this way everyone will know you're My disciples — if you love each other."

Jesus told the disciples that they would all be tempted to leave Him that very night. Peter boasted, "Even though all the rest leave You, I never will. I'm ready to go to prison and be put to death with You!"

Jesus said, "I tell you, Peter, this night, before the cock crows twice, you will deny knowing Me three times."

But Peter answered confidently, "Even if I had to *die* with You, I will never deny You." And all the other disciples agreed.

As they were eating together, Jesus took bread and blessed it, and broke it into pieces. As He gave it to His disciples, He said, "Take and eat, for this is My body which is broken for you." He meant that the bread was like His body, and represented it, because His body was soon to be broken, and crucified, and offered up on the cross for them.

Then He took some wine in a cup, and when He had thanked God He gave the cup to them and they all drank from it. And He said, "This wine is My blood, which is shed for the forgiveness of sins."

Jesus meant that the wine was like His blood, and represented it, because His blood was very soon to be shed, like the blood of the sacrifices at the altar, so that everyone who believed and trusted in Him would have their sins forgiven and be part of God's family.

Then Jesus told His disciples that they must meet together after He had been put to death, and eat the bread and drink the wine in the way He had shown them; and to remember Him as often as they did it.

This is the Communion, or Lord's Supper, that His disciples still observe. It was Jesus who told His followers to do this. Whenever Christians today see the broken bread in that Supper, they think of Jesus' body, wounded and nailed to the cross. And whenever they see the wine they think of His blood, poured out from the wounds in His hands and His side. Those who love Him will keep sharing this Supper until He comes to the earth again. Every time they eat it they think of the sins they've committed, and remember with thanksgiving that Jesus took the punishment for them on the cross; and they must repent of those sins and determine not to commit them anymore.

As they sat at the table, Jesus told His disciples not to be concerned that He would be taken away from them. He explained He was going to heaven, to make a place ready for them there. Jesus said, "If you love Me, you'll do what I tell you. I will ask the Father, and He will give you another Helper to be with you forever. The Helper is the Spirit of Truth. The people of the world can't accept Him, because they don't see Him or know Him. But you know Him. He lives with you, and He will be in you. I won't leave you all alone like orphans. I'll come back to you. Soon, the people in the world won't see Me anymore. But you will see Me. You will live because I live."

Jesus was promising that His Father would send the Holy Spirit into their hearts to make them remember and understand everything He had told them, and show them what to teach others. The Holy Spirit would stay with them, and be their Comforter, while Jesus was away from them. That promise is for His followers today, too.

Jesus said, "Don't be worried. Trust in God, and trust in Me. There are many rooms in my Father's house. I wouldn't be telling you this if it wasn't true. I'm going there to prepare a place for you. After I go and prepare a place for you, I'll come back. Then I'll take you with me, so you can be where I am. You already know the way to the place where I'm going."

Thomas said, "Lord, we don't know where You're going, so how can we know the way?"

Jesus told him, "I am the Way, the Truth, and the Life. The only way to the Father is through Me. If you really knew Me, you would know my Father too. But now you do know the Father, because you have seen Him."

Philip said, "Lord, show us the Father. That is all we need."

Jesus said, "Philip, I've been with you a long time, so you know Me now. I tell you, anyone who has seen Me has seen the Father too. So why are you asking, 'Show us the Father'? Don't you believe that I am in the Father and the Father is in Me? The things I've told you don't come from Me. The Father lives in Me, and He is doing His own work. You must believe Me when I say that I am in the Father and the Father is in Me. Or you can believe because of the miracles you've seen Me do."

Jesus then said, "I am the vine and you are the branches." He meant that He was like a vine, and the disciples were like branches growing out of the vine. Jesus said His Father took care of the good branches that bore fruit, and made them stronger, so they would bear more fruit. But the bad branches that bore no fruit were cut off and thrown into the fire. So if the disciples wanted to bear fruit — that is, if they wanted to do the things Jesus told them to do — they must keep on loving and obeying Him, for without His help they couldn't do anything that was good and pleasing to God.

When Jesus told the disciples that He had chosen them to bear fruit and do good things among the people, He said they must remember what He had already told them: that the people wouldn't love them for doing these things, but would hate them and persecute them.

"And now," Jesus said, "you're all sad because I'm to be taken away from you. But after I've risen from the dead I will see you again, and then you will be full of joy."

Jesus told them that when they asked anything from God, to ask it in His name and for His sake. Before that time His disciples had never prayed in this way, but now they were to do it, and God would always hear and answer their prayers when they prayed in Jesus' name, because Jesus was the One who was taking the punishment for their sins.

Then Jesus looked towards heaven and prayed for His disciples, and for everyone who would believe in Him by hearing the words His disciples preached. He prayed that they would be kept from sin, and would love each other. He said He wanted them to be with Him in heaven, where they could see His glory which His Father had given Him.

After this, Jesus and His disciples sang a hymn together, then they left the house where they'd eaten the Passover and went to the foot of the Mount of Olives, which was just across the Kidron Valley, very close to Jerusalem. There, they went into a garden called the garden of Gethsemane.

Jesus took Peter, James and John away from the others and told them something of how He felt about the ordeal ahead. Then He told all His disciples, "Sit here while I go over there and pray."

He went a little way from them, and knelt down and prayed, "*Abba*, Father, all things are possible for You. Remove this cup from Me. But You must do what You want, not what I want." Because He was being punished for the sins of the world, and knew that in a few hours He would be crucified, He was in agony, and His sweat was like drops of blood falling to the ground.

When Jesus got up from prayer and went back to His disciples, He found they were asleep. So He said, "Why are you all asleep? Get up and pray, in case you're tempted to do wrong."

Jesus went away again and prayed, and when He came back he found them asleep again. But when He came the third time, He said, "Get up, we have to go. It's time for the Son of Man to be handed over to sinful men. Look, the person who's going to betray Me is coming now."

Judas had been watching when Jesus went to the garden, and thought it the best time to betray Jesus. The priests had already paid him the thirty silver coins, so he went to the chief priests and elders and told them it was time, and they gave him a band of Temple guards to go with him and take Jesus prisoner. And now Judas was leading the men to the garden. Although Jesus knew it, He didn't run away, but waited to let them take Him, because He knew His time had come to die.

While He was still speaking to His disciples, and telling them that the person who would betray Him was near, Judas came with the band of men carrying swords, clubs and lanterns.

Judas had already given them a sign. "The man I kiss is Jesus. Take Him and hold Him tightly."

Then he went up to Jesus, and said, "Teacher," and kissed Him.

Jesus said, "Judas, do you betray Me with a kiss?"

Then the men caught hold of Jesus. When the disciples saw them take Jesus, they said to Him, "Lord, shall we fight them with swords?"

Peter had a short sword, and he drew it and struck a servant of the high priest, called Malchus, and cut off his ear. But Jesus said, "Put your sword back. If I wanted help, I could pray to My Father and ask Him to send Me thousands of angels to fight for Me and save Me from death. But how then could the words of the prophets come true, which say I am to die for the people?"

Then Jesus touched the servant's ear and healed it. Then He said to the men who had taken Him prisoner, "Have you come out with swords and clubs to take Me, as though I'm a criminal? When I sat in the Temple teaching, you did nothing to Me."

Then all His disciples were afraid, and they left Him and fled.

Matthew 26-27; Mark 14-15; Luke 22-23; John 18-19

Jesus is led before the high priest; Peter denies his Master; Jesus is brought before the council; He is condemned to death; He commits His mother to John's care; He dies on the cross.

THE MEN who took Jesus led Him away to Caiaphas who was the high priest that year. In the high priest's palace all the chief priests were gathered together with the scribes and the elders, waiting for Jesus to be brought to them.

Peter had followed Jesus, a good way off, hoping that no one would recognize him. When he came into the high priest's house he sat down among the servants by a fire burning there, because he wanted to see what was going to happen.

A young woman came to Peter, and said, "*You* were with Jesus of Galilee!"

Peter denied it, and said he wasn't. He went out on the porch, and the cock crowed. There another maid saw him, and said to the people who stood by, "This man was with Jesus of Nazareth."

Again Peter denied it. He said, "I don't know the man!"

After a while, one of the servants of the high priest, who was a relation of Malchus whose ear Peter had cut off, said, "Didn't I see you with Jesus in the garden?"

Peter denied it again, and the cock crowed the second time. Jesus turned and looked at Peter, and Peter remembered the words Jesus had spoken to him: "Before the cock crows twice, you will deny knowing Me three times." Then he went out and wept bitterly.

The high priest asked Jesus about His disciples, and about the words He preached. Jesus said, "I taught in the synagogues and in the Temple, where the Jews always go, and I've taught nothing in secret. Why do you ask Me? Ask the people who were listening. They know what I said."

When Jesus said this, one of the Temple officers slapped Him with the palm of his hand, and said, "Is this how you answer the high priest?"

Jesus said, "If I've spoken evil, tell the people whose job it is to punish Me; but if I've spoken correctly, why did you hit Me?"

The main court of the Jews, which tried people who disobeyed the Jewish law, used to meet in a room near the Temple. It was called the court, or council, of the Sanhedrim, and was made up of seventy men. The high priest was among them, with the chief priests and many of the scribes and elders. These men were the rulers of the Jews, and they punished people in various ways when they disobeyed the Law of Moses. But whenever they wanted to officially apply the death penalty, they had to ask permission from the Roman governor, because the Jews were servants to the Romans and weren't allowed to put anyone to death without the governor's consent. However, the Romans usually turned a blind eye to stoning. However, they would have feared a major riot if Jesus was stoned, which is why the Jewish leaders wanted the Romans to execute Jesus, rather than killing Him themselves.

As soon as it was morning, the men who had taken Jesus brought Him before the council. There, the chief priests, scribes and elders tried to find false witnesses to speak against Him. At last two false witnesses came, who told the court, "This man said, 'I'm able to destroy the Temple and build it up again in three days.'"

But Jesus didn't answer them.

Then the high priest stood up and said, "Are you going to say nothing?"

Jesus stayed silent.

Then the high priest said, "I ask You to tell us whether You are the Christ, the Son of God?"

Jesus answered, "I am. And I tell you, in the future you will see Me sitting on the right hand of God, and coming back to earth again in the clouds of heaven."

Then the high priest ripped his clothes in anger, and said, "Do we need any more witnesses against Him? You have heard the wicked blasphemy He speaks. What do you say His punishment should be?"

The men in the council said Jesus should be put to death. They spat in His face, and made fun of Him. Then they blindfolded Him and hit Him, saying, "Tell us, You Christ, who hit You."

After they had tied Jesus up securely, all the council rose and took Him to Pontius Pilate, the Roman governor. When they brought Jesus to Pilate's house they changed the charge of blasphemy against Him, because the governor wouldn't be interested in something to do with the Jews' religious laws, so they told Pilate instead, "We found this man teaching the Jews to rebel against the Romans, and telling them not to pay tribute to the Emperor, and saying that He Himself is Christ, a king."

Pilate asked Jesus, "Are You a king?"

Jesus answered, "I am, but My kingdom is not of this

world. If it was, My servants would fight to rescue Me."

Pilate said to the chief priests and to the Jews who had brought Him, "I can't find any fault with this man."

This made them even more angry, and they shouted out, "He stirs up the people to do wrong through all Judea, from Galilee to Jerusalem."

When Pilate heard them speak of Galilee, he asked if Jesus came from there. Then, after they told him that He had, Pilate sent Him to Herod, who was governor over that part of the land; for Herod was in Jerusalem at this time. This was Herod Antipas, the son of Herod the Great mentioned in the account of Jesus' birth. Herod Antipas had also ordered John the Baptist to be beheaded.

When Herod saw Jesus, he was glad, because for a long time he'd wanted to see Him, because he'd heard many things of Him, and he was probably hoping to see Jesus do some miracles. Herod asked Jesus many questions, but Jesus said nothing, while the chief priests and scribes stood by and angrily accused Him.

Then Herod with his soldiers made fun of Jesus, and put a purple robe on Him, because He'd said He was a king. Afterwards, Herod sent Jesus back to Pilate.

Pilate called the Jews together, with the chief priests and rulers, and said to them, "You've brought this man to me as someone who stirs up the people to do wrong. Having questioned Him in front of you, I can find no fault in Him. Neither has Herod. Nothing for which He ought to die has been proved against Him."

Every year, when the feast of the Passover was held in Jerusalem, if any of the Jews were in prison for disobeying the Romans, the Roman governor set one of them free. By tradition, he allowed the Jews to say which prisoner it should be. He did this to please them, and make them more willing to let the Romans rule over them.

There was at this time a Jew called Barabbas in prison. The people now began to ask the governor to do what he'd always done, and set one of the prisoners free.

Pilate said, "Which prisoner will it be? Barabbas, or Jesus, who is called the Christ?" He knew the Jewish leaders had only brought Jesus to be punished because they hated Him. While Pilate was speaking with them, his wife sent him a message that said, "Don't harm that innocent man. I've had a disturbing dream about Him."

But the chief priests persuaded the crowd of Jews to ask for Barabbas to be set free. Pilate asked them, "What shall I do with Jesus, who is called the Christ?"

They all shouted out, "Let Him be crucified."

Pilate said, "Why, what evil has He done?"

But they shouted out even more loudly, "Crucify Him!"

When Pilate saw he was unable to persuade the crowd to ask for Jesus to be set free, he took some water and washed his hands in front of the people, and said "I am not to blame for the death of this innocent man. You see to it."

Then all the Jews called back, "Let the blame be on us and on our children."

But washing his hands didn't take the blame from Pilate. The sin was in his heart, because he knew that although Jesus was innocent, he did not let Him go, but gave Him up to be crucified because he was afraid the Jews might be offended and want someone else for their governor. But of course Jesus had come to earth to die to take the punishment for our sins, and it was God's plan that this would happen.

The Romans, before they crucified a man, used to beat him

brutally. Jesus was stripped to the waist and His hands were tied to a low post in front of Him, to make Him bend forwards. While Jesus stood like this, He was beaten with rods and whips containing pieces of sharp metal.

Then the Roman soldiers, who were to crucify Jesus, took Him to a room in the governor's palace. There they mocked Him, as Herod had done before. They put a purple robe on Him and plaited a wreath of thorns which they pressed onto His head like a crown. Instead of a golden sceptre that kings held, they put a stick in His right hand. Then they bowed down before Him, pretending He was a king, and saying, "Hail, King of the Jews!" They spat at Him, and took the stick and hit Him on the head with it, then they put His own clothes back on Him.

After this punishment, Pilate hoped the Jews would be willing to let Jesus go. So he spoke to them again, and, "I'm bringing Him out to you, to tell you once again that I find no fault in Him."

Jesus was led out in front of the crowd, wearing the crown of thorns and the purple robe. Pilate said to them, "Look, here is the Man!"

But when the chief priests and the Jewish crowd saw Him, they shouted out, "Crucify Him! Crucify Him!"

Pilate said to them, "Take Him yourselves, then, and crucify Him, for I can find no fault in Him."

The Jewish leaders answered, "We have a law, and our law says He has to die, because He said He was the Son of God."

When Pilate heard them say this, he was even more afraid to put Jesus to death, and he said to Jesus, "Where do you come from?"

But Jesus said nothing.

Then Pilate said, "Won't You speak to me? Don't you

know I have the power to crucify You, and the power to let You go?"

Jesus said, "You can only do to Me what God will let you do."

From that moment on, Pilate tried to set Jesus free.

The emperor of Rome at that time was Tiberius Caesar. He was a jealous and cruel man, and Pilate was afraid of him. When the Jews realised Pilate wanted to set Jesus free, they shouted out, "If you let this man go, you're not Caesar's friend, because He said He was king instead of Caesar."

After they said this, Pilate was afraid to let Jesus go free in case the Jews told Caesar he had let Him go. So he changed his mind and agreed that Jesus should be crucified.

Judas Iscariot who had betrayed Jesus, when he saw that Jesus was going to die, was scared at what he'd done. He took the thirty silver coins back to the chief priests and elders, and told them, "I've sinned, because I've betrayed an innocent man."

They said, "What's that to us? It's your problem."

Then Judas threw the thirty silver coins onto the ground in the court of the Temple, and went away and hanged himself.

The chief priests took the silver coins, and said to each other, "It's against the law to put this money into the treasury at the Temple, because they were paid for a man who is to be put to death." So they used the money to buy a field to bury strangers in. It was known as the Potter's Field, and they buried Judas there.

The Roman soldiers took the purple robe off Jesus and put His own clothes back on Him, and led Him away to put Him to death. They forced a man called Simon, who came from

Cyrene to carry Jesus' cross. He was coming in from the country, and was the father of Alexander and Rufus. (Paul, writing to the Christians in Rome mentions someone called Rufus, so he may have been well known in the early church, which could be why Mark mentions him here — if it's the same man.)

A crowd of people followed Jesus, including women who mourned and wept for Him. But Jesus, turning to them told them not to weep for Him, but to weep for themselves and for their children, because of the sorrows that were coming to the country.

They brought Jesus to a place called Calvary, which was just outside of the gates of Jerusalem. There the Roman soldiers nailed His hands and His feet to the cross and crucified Him.

While the men were crucifying Him, Jesus prayed for them. "Father," He said, "forgive them, because they don't know what they're doing!" He meant they didn't know how great their sin was in crucifying Him, the Son of God.

They gave Jesus vinegar to drink, mixed with gall. This mixture was given to people who were crucified to make them feel their pains less. But when Jesus had tasted it He refused to drink it, because He was suffering those pains as a punishment for everyone, that they might be forgiven, and He was willing to bear every one of them. They crucified two thieves, one on each side of Jesus.

People who were crucified didn't die at once. They lived for many hours, hanging on the cross. So Jesus, although He was crucified in the morning, hung in agony until the afternoon. The soldiers who had crucified Him sat down and watched. They took His clothes and divided them among themselves, but they cast lots for who would get His coat.

Pilate ordered a sign to be fixed on the cross, above

Jesus' head. It said JESUS OF NAZARETH, THE KING OF THE JEWS. Many of the Jews and other passersby read these words, because the place where Jesus was crucified was near the city. The people who passed by felt no pity for Him, but shook their heads at Him, and said, "If You *are* the Son of God, come down from the cross!"

The chief priests and the scribes also made fun of Him, and said, "He trusted in God. Let God help Him now — if He will have Him!"

One of the two thieves who were crucified with Jesus spoke spitefully to Him, and said, "You are the Christ, so save Yourself, and us." But the other thief told him, "Don't you fear God, seeing you're dying? We deserve to die for what we've done, but this man has done nothing wrong." Then the thief said to Jesus, "Lord, remember me when You come into Your kingdom."

Jesus told him, "Today you will be with Me in Paradise." Jesus meant that the man's sins were forgiven, and as soon as he died, even on that very day, his soul would go to heaven, where Jesus Himself was going.

Jesus' mother, Mary, stood by the cross with the disciple John, who had leaned on Jesus at the table while they were eating the feast of the Passover. Because Jesus was going to die and leave his mother, Jesus wanted John to take care of her. So He told John to look after her as if she were his own mother. He also told His mother to let John be like her son. So John took Mary to his own home to look after her and give her everything she needed.

From midday (the sixth hour) there was darkness over all the land until three in the afternoon (the ninth hour). God sent that darkness because His Son was being put to death for the sins of the world.

Then Jesus called out in a loud voice, "My God, My God, why have You forsaken Me?" He said this because God seemed then to turn away from Him, displeased, as an earthly father turns away displeased from a child when they've disobeyed him. Yet Jesus had not disobeyed God. But everyone else has disobeyed God, and Jesus was taking the blame on Himself.

Therefore God turned away from Jesus as though Jesus Himself had sinned. When Jesus saw this, He cried out because it grieved Him more than all His sufferings.

One of the men standing near, when he heard Jesus call out, ran and took a sponge and filled it with vinegar. Putting it on a reed he lifted it up to Jesus' mouth and gave it to Him to drink. When Jesus had taken the vinegar, He said, "It is finished."

He meant that the work He had come to do, and the punishment He had come to bear for the sins of the world, were finished. And He bowed His head and died. Then the curtain, called the veil, which hung in the Temple, was torn into two pieces, torn from the top to the bottom. The curtain was there to separate the people from God, but now that Jesus has died, anyone can come to God without fear of punishment, if they trust in Jesus.

The earth shook, the rocks were broken, and the graves were opened, and many of those people who, while they lived, had served the Lord, arose and came out of their graves after Jesus Himself had risen from the dead; and they went into Jerusalem, and were seen by many of the people there.

When the Roman soldiers who were watching Jesus saw these things happening, they were very afraid, and the centurion said, "Surely this man was the Son of God."

Matthew 27-28; Mark 15-16; Luke 23-24; John 19-21; 1 Corinthians 15; Acts 1

The two crucified thieves are killed; Joseph of Arimathea buries Jesus; a guard is set at the tomb; an angel rolls the stone away from the door; Jesus rises from the dead; He appears to His disciples and ascends to heaven.

THE JEWISH leaders who were in the city hadn't heard that Jesus was already dead, and because the next day was the Sabbath they were unwilling to let the bodies hang on the cross during the Sabbath. So they asked Pilate to kill Jesus and the two thieves who were crucified with Him, so they could be taken down and buried before the Sabbath began.

So Pilate gave the order to the Roman soldiers, and they broke the legs of the two thieves to kill them. In that way, their legs would no longer support their bodies and in their weakened condition they would not be able to breathe. But when they came to Jesus and saw He was already dead, they didn't break His legs, but one of the soldiers pierced His side with a spear, and blood and water came out.

Before the first Passover in Egypt, Moses said that the sacrificed lamb must not have its legs broken. John the Baptist had said, when Jesus came to him to be baptised, "Look, the Lamb of God. He takes away the sins of the world!" And like the sacrificed lamb, when Jesus was crucified, not one of His legs was broken, because Jesus was the Passover Lamb, sacrificed to pay the penalty for our sins.

Near the place where Jesus was crucified there was a garden, and in the garden was a new tomb in which no one had ever been buried. It was a cave cut out of the rock, belonging to a rich man called Joseph who came from the town of Arimathea.

Joseph was a disciple of Jesus, although he had kept it a secret because he was afraid of the Jewish leaders. But now, after Jesus was dead, he and a man called Nicodemus went to Pilate and begged for Jesus' body. Then Pilate ordered the body to be given to them for burial.

Joseph and Nicodemus (Nicodemus had earlier visited Jesus at night) took Jesus' body down from the cross and wrapped it in new, fine linen that Joseph had bought, and laid it in the tomb, and rolled a huge, round stone to seal the entrance.

Mary Magdalene, and Mary the mother of James the disciple, were near the tomb and saw where they laid Jesus. Then they went away to rest during the Sabbath, planning to come back the day after with spices and ointments to put on His body. They were doing this because the Jews, when they buried their dead, used to prepare the bodies in that way, but because of the Sabbath there was no time to do it then.

After Jesus was buried, the chief priests and the Pharisees went to Pilate, and said, "Sir, we remember that while that deceiver was still alive, He said, 'After three days I will rise again.' So we beg you to have the tomb guarded and made safe until the third day, in case His disciples come in the night and steal Him away, then tell the people He has risen from the dead."

Pilate said, "You will have soldiers to guard the tomb. Go and make it as secure as you can."

So they went and made the tomb secure, setting soldiers

to guard it, and sealing the stone that was rolled to the door.

But that night the angel of the Lord came from heaven and rolled the stone back from the door, and sat on it. His face was bright like lightning, and his clothes were as white as snow. The soldiers shook in fear, and were weak and helpless, like dead men. They left the tomb and went back to Jerusalem.

Very early in the morning, as soon as it began to be light on the first day of the week (Sunday), Mary Magdalene and the other Mary and Salome went to the tomb, with the spices they'd already prepared. On the way, they said to each other, "Who will roll the stone away for us from the entrance to the tomb?"

The stone was very large, but when they came to the tomb they found it had already been rolled away. Going into the tomb they saw the angel dressed in white, and they were afraid. The angel said, "Don't be afraid. You're looking for Jesus who was crucified. He's not here. He is risen. Look at the place where they laid Him. Now go and tell His disciples that He is risen from the dead, and that He will go before you into Galilee, and you'll see Him there."

They went out quickly and fled from the tomb with fear mixed with great gladness, and ran to tell His disciples. As they went, Jesus met them and spoke to them, saying, "Rejoice." They went to Him and held Him by the feet, and worshipped Him. He said, "Don't be afraid, but tell My followers to go into Galilee and see Me there."

The women hurried and told everything to the eleven apostles, and to the other disciples who were with them. And Peter and John, when they heard what the women said, hurried to the tomb. They ran together, but John outran Peter and reached the tomb first. Bending down and looking in at the entrance, he saw the linen clothes Jesus had worn, lying there, but he didn't go in.

But Peter, when he came, went into the tomb and saw the linen clothes. The napkin which had been wrapped about the head of Jesus, wasn't lying with the linen clothes, but was folded up by itself. Then John went in, and he saw and believed that Jesus was risen. Until then, the disciples didn't grasp the words Jesus had spoken to them while He was alive, when He said that after three days He would rise from the dead. Then the disciples went away to their own homes.

After Jesus had risen from the dead, some of the soldiers who had guarded the tomb went to the chief priests and told them what had happened. Then the chief priests and elders gave them a large amount of money, and said, "Go and tell the people that Jesus' disciples came at night and stole Him away while you were sleeping. If the governor hears about it and wants to punish you for sleeping (because Roman soldiers were put to death if they slept while on guard), we will persuade him to pardon you."

So the soldiers took the money and did as the chief priests told them. That was why many Jews at that time believed that the disciples of Jesus came and stole Him away in the night, while the soldiers were asleep.

On the first day of the week (Sunday), the day Jesus had risen from the dead, two of His disciples were walking together to a village called Emmaus which was only a few miles from Jerusalem. They were talking with each other about everything that had happened. While they were talking, Jesus came near and walked with them. But He was changed so that they didn't recognise Him.

Jesus said to them, "What are you talking about as you walk? And why are you sad?"

One of Jesus' followers whose name was Cleopas, said, "Are You a stranger in Jerusalem? Haven't You heard what's happened there in past few days?"

Jesus said, "What has happened?"

They said, "About Jesus of Nazareth, who was a prophet, and did great miracles before all the people; how the chief priests and the rulers have taken Him and crucified Him. But we hoped He was the one to set the Children of Israel free from the Romans. Today is the third day since He was put to death."

(Jesus rose on the third day. The day of the crucifixion was Friday, which the Jews counted as day one. Saturday – the Sabbath – was day two, and the third day was our Sunday. Jesus, in the way the Jews reckoned time, was dead for three days, even though all but the Saturday consisted of only a few hours. This means that Jesus was dead for about thirty-six hours, which is a short enough time for His followers to plan to anoint His body.)

Then they said, "And now some of the women who belong to our group of followers, who went to the tomb early this morning, have amazed us by saying Jesus' body wasn't there. The said they saw a vision of angels who told them He was alive. And some of His followers who were with us went to the tomb and found it just as the women had said. But they didn't see Him."

Then Jesus told the two disciples that the things which had happened in Jerusalem seemed strange to them, because they didn't understand what the prophets had written. For wasn't it to be expected, Jesus asked, from what the prophets had said about the Christ, the Messiah, that He would be put to death, and afterwards rise from the dead and go up to heaven? Then Jesus explained what was written about Himself in the Scriptures. But still the two disciples didn't realise it was Jesus.

As they came near the village to which they were going, Jesus began to walk on ahead, as though He was continuing his journey. But they said to Him, "Come and stay with us tonight, for it's nearly evening and the daylight has almost gone."

So Jesus went into their house. While they were eating supper, Jesus took bread, and after thanking God for it, He broke it and gave it to them. As He was doing this they recognised Him; and suddenly He disappeared.

Then the two disciples said to each other, "When He talked to us on the way here it was like fire burning in our hearts as He explained what the prophets have written."

They hurried back to Jerusalem and found the eleven apostles gathered together, and other followers of Jesus with them. The two disciples told everyone how they'd seen Jesus and talked with Him, and how they'd not known who He was until He was breaking the bread.

While they were telling this, Jesus appeared, standing in the room with them. He said, "Peace be with you."

But they were frightened, for they thought it was a ghost. So Jesus said, "Why are you upset, and why are you so afraid? Look at My hands and My feet. Touch Me, and see it's really Me. A ghost doesn't have flesh and bones."

Then He showed them His hands and His feet with the marks of the nails in them. And while they could hardly believe for joy, He said to them, "Do you have any food here?"

They gave Jesus a piece of a cooked fish and some honey still in the comb, and He ate it there in the room.

Jesus said, "I told you while I was still with you that everything must be fulfilled which is written about Me in the Scriptures."

Then He helped His followers understand those parts of the Scriptures which said He would die for the people, and rise again from the dead. For although they were familiar with those parts of Scripture, they had never, until now, been able to understand them properly.

Jesus said, "That is what was written about Me, and so it was necessary for me to die, and rise from the dead on the third day, so the people of all the countries in the world can now be told how I have died for *them* too. If they repent and believe, and put their trust in Me, they will have their sins forgiven. Whoever believes in Me and is baptized, will be saved; but the person who doesn't believe will be lost."

Thomas, one of the disciples, wasn't with the others when Jesus came. When they told him they had seen the Lord, Thomas said, "Unless I can see the marks of the nails in His hands, and put my hand in the wound the spear made in His side, I won't believe it really was Jesus."

Eight days later the disciples were again meeting together. This time Thomas was with them, and the doors of the room were locked. Then Jesus came and stood there with them, and said "Peace be with you."

Then He said to Thomas, "Put out your finger and touch My hands, and put your hand into My side. Have no more doubts, but believe that I have risen."

When Thomas heard His voice and knew it was Jesus, he said, "My Lord and my God."

Jesus said to him, "Thomas, because you've seen Me you have believed. But I tell you, there are great blessings for those who are willing to believe, even though they haven't seen Me."

After this, Jesus showed Himself again to His disciples, this time by the Sea of Galilee. It happened like this. Peter,

Thomas, Nathaniel, James and John were there, with two more of Jesus' disciples.

Peter told them, "I'm going fishing."

They said, "We'll go with you."

They got into a boat and sailed out on the water, but that night they caught nothing. When it was early morning, Jesus stood on the shore. But the disciples didn't know it was Jesus. He called out to them, "Do you have any food?"

They called back, "No."

Jesus said, "Throw the net on the right side of the boat and you'll catch some."

They did as Jesus said and were unable to pull up the net, because there were so many fish caught in it.

John said to Peter, "It's the Lord!"

When Peter heard it was the Lord, he fastened his fisherman's coat around him and jumped into the water to get quickly to the shore. The other disciples came in the boat, dragging the net full of fish. As soon as they reached land they saw a fire burning on the shore, and fish on it, and bread.

Jesus said, "Bring some of the fish you've just caught."

Then Peter helped pull the net to land, and it was full of fish: a hundred and fifty-three. Although there were so many fish, the net wasn't broken.

Jesus said to them, "Come and eat."

And none of the disciples dared to ask, "Who are You?" because they knew it was the Lord Jesus. This was the third time Jesus had shown Himself to them since He'd risen from the dead.

On another occasion Jesus met his disciples on a mountain in Galilee, where He'd told them to meet Him. When they saw Jesus they worshipped Him, and He said, "God has given Me all power, both in heaven and in earth. Go and preach the good news to the people of every country, baptizing them in the name of the Father, and of the Son, and of the Holy Spirit. Teach them to do all the things I've taught you."

Jesus didn't only show Himself to His disciples, but the apostle Paul writes that on one occasion He was seen by more than five hundred people who believed in Him.

Forty days after Jesus had risen from the dead, He met His disciples again in Jerusalem. When He'd talked with them, and told them to stay in Jerusalem until the Holy Spirit was sent on them, He told them to go with Him to the Mount of Olives.

There, He lifted up His hands and blessed them. And while He blessed them, He was carried up into a cloud out of their sight, to heaven. And while the disciples continued to stare upwards, two angels in white clothing came and stood by them. The angels said, "Men of Galilee, why are you standing here, staring up into heaven? One day Jesus will come down again, in the clouds, just as you've seen Him go up into heaven."

Then Jesus' followers went back to Jerusalem, with great joy, praising God.

The Acts of the Apostles

Acts 1-5

(Luke is believed to be the writer of Acts, as well as his own Gospel)

The apostles return to Jerusalem; Matthias is chosen in place of Judas; the Holy Spirit is sent on the disciples; Peter heals a lame man at the Temple; an angel opens the prison doors and sets the apostles free; Ananias and Sapphira die; the apostles are imprisoned and beaten.

AFTER Jesus was taken up to heaven, the apostles were all together in an upstairs room in Jerusalem, where they prayed and gave thanks to God. About 120 other believers were with them. These are the apostles who were there: Peter, John, James, Andrew, Philip, Thomas, Bartholomew, Matthew, James (the son of Alphaeus), Simon (the Zealot), and Judas (the son of James). Some women, including Mary the mother of Jesus, and His brothers were also there.

Peter stood up and said to everyone, "The words David prophesied about Judas must come true, for in the Psalms we read that one of us would no longer be an apostle, and someone else would take his place. So, of those of you who have believed in Jesus, and been with Him since He was baptized by John until He was taken up to heaven, one of you must be chosen to go with us to tell the people about Jesus, and tell them that He's risen from the dead."

The apostles agreed with Peter, and they took Joseph and Matthias, and prayed, "Lord, You can see everyone's heart, so please show us which of these two men You have chosen."

Then they cast lots to know who it would be, and the lot showed Matthias to be the one. From then on, he was counted with the eleven apostles.

When it was the day for the Feast of Pentecost, the disciples were all together in one room. Suddenly they heard a sound like a rushing wind from heaven, which filled the house where they were sitting. Then what seemed like tongues of fire were everywhere, and one of these flames rested on the head of each disciple.

Then the Holy Spirit came into them, as Jesus had promised, and they began to speak in languages they had never understood before, telling of the great things God had done.

There were some Jews in Jerusalem who had come from the countries where those languages were spoken. When they heard the disciples, they were amazed, and said, "Don't all these men come from Galilee? So how are they able to speak the languages of our own countries?"

Some people, who didn't understand the words the disciples were speaking, made fun of them, and said they were drunk.

So Peter stood up with the other apostles, and said, "These men aren't drunk, but God has sent His Holy Spirit into them. So listen, everyone, to what I have to say. Jesus of Nazareth did great miracles among you that showed that God had sent Him, but you took Him and put Him to death because you didn't like the things He said and did. But He's risen from the dead, for it's written in the Scriptures that God would raise Him up. And we, His apostles, have seen Him since He rose. So you unbelievers, and all the Children of Israel, will surely know that Jesus, whom you crucified, is the Messiah, the Saviour who has to come into the world."

When the Jews heard these words they were filled with sorrow for what they'd done, and they said to Peter and the other apostles, "Brothers, what can we do?"

Peter told them, "Repent of your sins, and be baptized, and the Holy Spirit will also be given to you. God has promised to send Him to you, and your children, and to all who hear and obey Him when He calls."

Then a huge number of people believed and put their trust in the Lord Jesus, and about three thousand people were baptized that day. The new believers met together with the apostles, and with the rest of the disciples. They listened to the teaching of the apostles, shared the new Christian life together, ate together, and prayed together. Those who had money gave to those who had none. Then they went to the Temple to worship, being full of joy. Every day, others who repented and believed, came to the apostles and were baptized.

One afternoon, Peter and John went up to the Temple to pray. A poor man, who had been lame ever since he was born, was carried every day by his friends and placed by the gate of the Temple called the Beautiful Gate. There, he would ask for money or gifts from the people who came to worship. This man, seeing Peter and John about to go into the Temple, asked them for money.

Peter, looking at him closely, said, "Look at us."

The man looked, because he expected they had something to give him. Then Peter said, "I don't have any silver or gold, but I do have something to give you. In the name of Jesus Christ of Nazareth, stand up and walk!"

Then Peter held onto the man's right hand and lifted him up, and immediately the man's feet and ankles were made strong. Jumping up, he went with them into the Temple, walking and leaping and praising God.

Everyone who saw him recognised him as the man who used to sit begging at the Beautiful Gate. And they were amazed, and ran to find the apostles.

When Peter saw them all standing there, he said, "Why are you surprised by this? Why do you look so closely at us, as if *we* had made this man walk? It is by faith in the Name of Jesus that this man has been healed. Therefore tell God you're sorry for your sins, and believe and trust in Jesus, so when He comes again at the Judgment day, your sins will be forgiven."

There was a Jewish sect called Sadducees. They didn't believe there would ever be a Judgment day, or even that the dead would rise from their graves. Some of these Sadducees belonged to the Council of the Sanhedrim, and were rulers over the Jews when it came to religious matters.

While Peter and John were speaking in the Temple, the Sadducees hurried there in anger, because they heard that the apostles were preaching about Jesus and the resurrection — that is, the rising from the dead. So they put them in prison to keep them until the next day, for it was now the evening.

However, so many people had been listening to what Peter and John had been saying before they were put in prison, that about five thousand of them believed in Jesus, so there were now thousands of new Christians.

The next day the council met together. When they brought in Peter and John, they asked them, "By what power did you heal the lame man?"

Peter said, "Rulers of the people, and elders of Israel, you're wondering how the lame man was healed. It was by the power of Jesus of Nazareth, the Man you killed on a cross, but we know is alive again. For though you thought nothing of Jesus while He was on earth, God has made Him to be the ruler over us all. There's no one in the entire world who can save us from being punished by God for our sins, except Jesus."

When the rulers realised Peter and John were poor and uneducated men, yet weren't afraid to speak in front of them, they were surprised. When they saw the man who'd been healed standing near them, they were unable to deny what the apostles had done. Telling the apostles to wait outside, they said to each other, "What are we to do with these men? Everyone in Jerusalem will soon know they've done a great miracle, and we won't be able to contradict it. But to stop the news spreading further, let's tell them we'll punish them if they keep preaching to the people."

So they called Peter and John, and ordered them not to say anything about Jesus. But Peter and John told them, "Whether it's right for us to obey you rather than God, you must judge for yourselves. But we can't help teaching the people about Jesus, and telling them about the things we've heard Him speak, and seen Him do."

The rulers still threatened to punish them, but in the end they had to let them go because they couldn't prove they had done anything wrong.

As soon as they were let go, Peter and John went to the apostles who were with the other believers, and explained what the rulers had told them. Then they all prayed together, "Lord, help us not to be afraid to preach the good news of Jesus; and please give us power to do miracles in Jesus' name."

When they'd finished praying, the building they were in was shaken. In this way God let them know He'd heard their prayer and would give them what they asked Him for. Then the apostles went out and preached to the people again, unafraid of what the rulers could do to them.

Many more Jews heard them and believed, and all the believers met together, helping and loving each other. Those who had houses or land sold them, and brought the money from the sale to the apostles, so they could use it to help the believers who were poor.

A man called Ananias, and Sapphira his wife, had some land which they sold, but they agreed together that they would only bring some of the money to the apostles, and pretend they'd brought it all. They wanted to make the apostles believe they were true disciples of Jesus, while in their hearts they didn't really know Him as their Saviour. But God told Peter what they were doing.

When Ananias came with the money and told Peter this lie, Peter said, "Ananias, wasn't the land your own before it was sold, so you didn't *have* to sell it? And wasn't the money your own after it was sold, to *keep* if you wanted it? Why have you let Satan tempt you to lie to the Holy Spirit?"

Peter said this because the Holy Spirit was with Peter and the other apostles, helping them teach the disciples and set up Christ's kingdom on earth.

Then Peter told Ananias that in lying to the Holy Spirit, he was lying to God, because the Holy Spirit is God. (Not God the Father, nor God the Son, but God the Holy Spirit, the Three in One, known as the Trinity.)

As soon as Peter had said this, Ananias fell down dead. And when the disciples saw he was dead, the young men who were there took him and put grave clothes on him, and carried him out and buried him.

About three hours later, his wife, Sapphira, who didn't know what had happened, came to the house where the disciples were. Peter asked her, "Tell me, was the money your husband brought to us all you got from the sale of the land?"

She said, "Yes, all of it."

Then Peter said to her, "Why did you both agree to try and deceive the Spirit of the Lord? Look, the men are here who have just buried your husband, and they will also carry you out."

Then she fell down at Peter's feet and died. The young men came in and carried her out and buried her with her husband.

Everyone who heard this was really afraid, so no one else dared try to deceive the apostles as Ananias and Sapphira had done.

When the apostles preached and did miracles, many people believed in the Risen Saviour, both men and women. They brought out sick people on mats and mattresses, placing them in the streets, so even if Peter wasn't close enough to touch them, at least his shadow could fall on them as he passed by, to make them well. Crowds of people came from the towns and villages around Jerusalem, bringing family members and friends who were sick or who were possessed by evil spirits. They were all healed.

This made the high priest and the Sadducees angry at the apostles. They caught hold of them and put them in the common prison. But in the night, the angel of the Lord opened the prison doors and brought them out, and said, "Go up to the Temple and preach the good news of Jesus to the people."

So, early in the morning they went up to the Temple and preached there. But the high priest and the Sadducees, who didn't know what the angel had done, called the council together and sent to the prison to have the apostles brought to them. The officers went to the prison, but of course they weren't there.

They came back to the council and said, "The prison was sealed shut, and the guards were keeping watch in front of the doors, but the men you sent us for weren't there."

The rulers in the council wondered what this could mean. But while they were still wondering about it, a messenger came and told them, "The men you put in prison are standing in the Temple, and they're teaching the people!"

Then the officers went and caught hold of the apostles, but without doing them any harm in case the people who were listening to them became angry. When they brought them before the council, the high priest asked them, "Didn't we order you to stop speaking about Jesus? But you've disobeyed us."

Then Peter and the other apostles said, "We have to obey God, not men. You killed Jesus on the cross, but He's been raised up again by God, as a Saviour, to give the Jews new and repenting hearts, and forgive their sins. And we, His apostles, are here to tell you about it."

When the high priest and the rulers heard what the apostles said, they were furious with them, and discussed among themselves how they could put them to death. Then one of the rulers stood up, a Pharisee called Gamaliel, who was held in high regard by all the Jews. He ordered the apostles to wait outside for a little while.

When they had gone, Gamaliel said, "Rulers of Israel, you must be careful what you do to these men. Some time ago a man called Theudas rose up, claiming that he was some great person. About four hundred men followed him and did whatever he told them to do. But before long he was killed, and all who had obeyed him went their own ways. Later, another man, called Judas, from Galilee, persuaded many people to follow him, but he also died, and those who had gone with him were scattered. And now I say you should let these men alone and don't do them any harm. If what they teach is not the truth, it will quickly come to nothing. But if God has sent them to speak to the people, you won't be able to stop them. If you try to stop them, you'll be fighting against God."

The men in the council agreed with what Gamaliel said, but before they agreed to let the apostles go, they had them beaten, and once again ordered them to stop preaching,. Then the apostles went out of the council rejoicing that they were allowed to suffer pain for Jesus' sake.

By now they understood that Jesus didn't come to be an earthly king, so they would not be made rich and great by preaching His gospel (gospel means good news), but would stay poor and be persecuted as He was, but they knew they would be rewarded when Jesus took them to heaven.

Acts 6-9

Seven men are chosen as special helpers; Stephen is stoned; the disciples flee to other countries; Philip preaches in Samaria; he baptizes the Ethiopian official; Saul is converted and preaches the gospel; Peter heals Aeneas who was paralyzed, and raises Dorcas from the dead.

WHEN the believers who had houses or lands sold them and brought the money to the apostles to use to give help to the poor, there were some poor Greek Jewish widows among the believers, who complained that their share of the help wasn't being given to them. So the apostles called all the disciples together and said, "It's wrong for us to stop preaching the gospel to attend to giving out money and food. So choose seven men from among yourselves who are honest and sensible, and full of the Holy Spirit. Let them take the money and see that it's distributed fairly. If you do this, we can spend our time preaching, and praying to God."

This pleased the disciples, and they chose seven men for this work. They were Stephen, Philip, Prochorus, Nicanor, Timon, Parmenas, and Nicolaus, who was a convert from Antioch. The disciples brought these seven men to the apostles, who prayed for them, that God would help them and give them wisdom in the work they were chosen to do.

When the apostles had prayed for them they laid their hands on the heads of each one, as they did to everyone they sent out to work and preach among the people.

After this, many were baptized, and large numbers of the

priests believed. Stephen, one of the seven chosen men, not only helped the poor, but preached to the people and did great miracles among them.

Then some of the Jews who refused to believe in Jesus, were angry and dragged Stephen before the council. They brought false witnesses to accuse him, who said, "This man never stops speaking bad words against the Temple and God's law."

So the high priest asked Stephen, "Is this true?"

Everyone sitting in the council meeting began staring at Stephen. His face looked like the face of an angel as he stood there.

Then Stephen said, "My Jewish fathers and brothers, please listen to what I have to say. A long time ago God spoke to our father Abraham and told him to go away from the land where he was born, and where he was then living, to another land God said He would show him. Then Abraham left his own land and came into the land of Canaan, where we now are. God promised to give this land to Abraham and to his descendants after he died. God also said Abraham's descendants would live in a country (Egypt) that wasn't theirs, for four hundred years, and the people there would treat them very cruelly. Yet God told Abraham He would punish the people who treated them like that, and afterwards He would bring Abraham's descendants back here, to what was then the land of Canaan.

"God made a covenant, or agreement, with Abraham and his descendants, and promised to be their God. He gave Abraham a son, who was called Isaac. Isaac had a son called Jacob; and Jacob had twelve sons, who were called the twelve great ancestors of our people, and Joseph was one of these brothers. His brothers, because they were jealous of him, sold him to the Ishmaelites, who took him to Egypt.

But God was with Joseph and caused Pharaoh, the king of Egypt, to accept him; and after a time Pharaoh made Joseph governor over Egypt.

"Then there was a great famine in Egypt and Canaan, and Joseph's brothers had nothing for themselves or their families to eat. But Jacob, their father, heard there was corn in Egypt, and he sent them there to try to buy food. When they got there, Joseph recognized them, but he said nothing to them, but told Pharaoh about them. Then Joseph told them to go home and come back to Egypt with their father Jacob, their wives, and their children. Jacob (who was also called Israel) came to Egypt and died there of old age, and then Joseph and his brothers eventually died there. Their bodies were taken back to Canaan to be buried in a tomb Abraham had bought from the sons of Hamor in Shechem.

"After many years their descendants grew and grew in number. Then another king ruled over Egypt who knew nothing about Joseph. This king was cruel to the Israelites and ordered his servants to take their baby boys and kill them to keep their numbers down.

"This is when Moses was born. He was very beautiful and his mother loved him, and she hid him for three months so the Egyptians couldn't find him and kill him. When she could hide him no longer, she put him in a basket by the river where Pharaoh's daughter found him. She felt sorry for him and took him home to bring him up as her own son; and he was educated in all the Egyptian culture and learning.

"But when Moses was forty years old he went out to visit his brothers, the Children of Israel. When he saw an Egyptian treat one of them cruelly, he killed the Egyptian and hid his body in the sand. Moses thought the Children of Israel would understand that God had sent him to set them free from the Egyptians. But they didn't understand. When

Pharaoh heard what Moses had done, he tried to kill him, but Moses fled to the land of Midian, where Pharaoh couldn't find him.

"After Moses had been in Midian for forty years he saw a flame of fire in a bush on Mount Sinai, but the bush wasn't burned up. When Moses saw it he was amazed. As he went to look at it more closely, God spoke to him out of the bush, and said, 'I am the God of your fathers, the God of Abraham, and the God of Isaac, and the God of Jacob.'

"Moses trembled and hid his face, because he was afraid to look at God. God told him He had seen the suffering of the Children of Israel, and was going to rescue them. Then God told Moses to go and bring the Children of Israel out of Egypt. He put Moses in charge of them.

"Moses did as God told him. He went to Egypt, and when he had called down great punishments on Pharaoh and his people, he brought the Children of Israel out of Egypt, going through the Red Sea; and afterwards led them for forty years through the desert. It is Moses," Stephen said, "who received God's laws on Mount Sinai to teach them to our fathers. But our fathers wouldn't obey Moses. They tried to stop him ruling over them, and said they wanted to go back to Egypt.

"While Moses was on Mount Sinai, the people asked Aaron to make an idol for them, saying, 'As for Moses, the man who brought us up out of Egypt, we don't know what's happened to him.'

"So Aaron used their jewellery to make a golden calf, and they offered sacrifices to it and worshipped it."

After Stephen had given this speech to the rulers in the council, and told them about the sinfulness of their ancestors, he told them, "You are like them. How many prophets did they *not* persecute? They killed those who were sent to tell them that Jesus was coming, and now *you* have killed the Holy One Himself."

When the men in the council heard this, they were furious with Stephen, and ground their teeth like wild beasts. But Stephen was looking up towards heaven where he saw a glorious light, and Jesus standing at the right hand of God. So he said, "I see the heavens opened, and the Son of Man standing at God's right hand."

Then they shouted out against him, and blocked up their ears so that they couldn't hear what he was saying. Then they brought Stephen out of the city to stone him.

It was a custom that whenever a man or woman was stoned to death by the Jews, the people who had given evidence against them always threw the first stone. And so the false witnesses who had spoken against Stephen threw the first stones at him. They took off their outer clothing so they could use their arms more freely, and they put their clothes by the feet of a young man called Saul, for him to keep them safe until they were ready to put them on again.

While they were stoning Stephen, he kneeled on the ground, and prayed, "Lord, forgive them for this sin." And then he died.

After this, there was a great persecution against the believers. But some believers took Stephen's body, and mourned over him, and buried him. As for Saul, the young man who'd kept the clothes of the witnesses, he went to every house to find those who followed Jesus. When he found them, he took them, both men and women, and put them in prison. So the believers fled from Jerusalem to different parts of the land, and to other countries. Wherever they went, they passed on the good news of Jesus to the people. It was because of this persecution that the good news of Jesus spread quickly around the different countries.

<><><>

Philip, one of the seven men chosen to help distribute the food fairly (not the apostle Philip), went to the city of Samaria. This may have been Sychar, where Jesus had earlier met the woman by the well and told her about living water, and stayed in the town with the people for three days. So some people in the area had probably seen Jesus and heard Him speaking to them, and knew who He was.

Philip now preached to the people there. They listened to him and saw the miracles he did, as unclean spirits, shouting loudly, came out when He commanded them, and people who were sick, or paralyzed, or lame, were made well. So there was great happiness in the city and many men and women believed and were baptized.

There was a man called Simon at Samaria who tricked the people by claiming he could do things for them by magic. Everyone listened to him, and said, "This man has power given to him by God."

But when Philip preached the gospel in that city, and many believed and were baptized, Simon came and said he also believed, and asked to be baptized. So Philip baptized him. Afterwards, Simon stayed with Philip, amazed at the miracles he did.

When the apostles who were still in Jerusalem heard this, they sent Peter and John to Samaria to see what exactly was happening there. When they got there, they prayed that the Holy Spirit would be given to the new believers. Then they laid their hands on the heads of those people, and God sent His Holy Spirit into them.

When Simon saw that this was how the Holy Spirit was given to people who believed, he went to the apostles and offered them money if they gave him power, by laying on of his hands, to bring down God's Holy Spirit from heaven. But

Peter told Simon he'd done wrong in thinking that money could buy what God gave to those who loved Him.

He said to Simon, "Repent of your sin, and ask to be forgiven, for I can see you're still a sinful man, and a servant of Satan."

Then Simon said, "Pray to the Lord for me, that He won't punish me."

An angel of the Lord spoke to Philip, and told him to leave Samaria and go through the desert on the road to the city of Gaza. Philip obeyed, and went. As he was going, he met a man from the country of Ethiopia, who was a eunuch, an important official under Candace, the queen of Ethiopia. He took care of all the queen's treasure, and was travelling that way. He had been to Jerusalem to worship at the Temple, and now he was sitting in his chariot, reading the Scriptures on his way home. The part he was reading was where the prophet Isaiah told the Children of Israel that a Saviour was coming to the world to die for their sins.

When Philip saw the queen's official, the Holy Spirit said, "Go to the chariot and talk to him."

So Philip ran, and as he got close to the chariot he heard the Ethiopian official reading aloud the words the prophet Isaiah had written. Philip said, "Do you understand what you're reading?"

The queen's official answered, "How can I, unless someone explains it to me?"

He asked Philip to come and sit with him in the chariot. Philip did so, and the Ethiopian official said, "Please tell me what the prophet meant when he wrote these words? Was he was speaking about himself or about some other man?"

Then Philip explained the meaning of the prophecy, and told the Ethiopian about Jesus. As they continued on their journey, they came to a place where there was water, and the queen's official said, "Look, here's some water. What is there to keep me from being baptized?"

Philip said, "If you believe with all your heart, you can certainly be baptized."

The Ethiopian official answered, "I believe that Jesus Christ is the Son of God."

Then he ordered the chariot to stop, and they went down into the water, both Philip and the Ethiopian official, and Philip baptized him. When they came up again the Holy Spirit took Philip away, so the official never saw him again.

The queen's official continued his journey back to Ethiopia, very happy, because he'd heard about Jesus and was now one of His disciples. Philip found himself in a city called Azotus, and from there he preached in all the towns on his way to Caesarea.

After the stoning of Stephen, Saul was full of anger and hatred to the believers. He went to the high priest at Jerusalem and asked for letters to the rulers of the synagogues in the city of Damascus, so if he found any believers there, he could arrest them, men and women, and take them back to Jerusalem to be punished. The high priest gave him the letters he asked for, and he set out for Damascus.

When Saul was near Damascus, suddenly a great light shone down from heaven, and Jesus appeared to him. Saul was afraid, and fell on the ground. He heard a voice saying, "Saul, Saul, why are you persecuting Me?"

Saul said, "Who are You, Lord?"

The voice said, "I am Jesus, the One you are persecuting."

Jesus was saying that when Saul persecuted His disciples, it was the same as if he persecuted Him.

Jesus said, "Get up and go into the city, and there you will be told what you must do."

The men who were with Saul stayed silent. They heard the voice, but couldn't understand the words. When Saul stood up he was unable to see, because the bright light had blinded him. The people with him led him by the hand, and brought him to Damascus. He was blind for three days, and didn't eat or drink.

There was a man called Ananias living in Damascus at that time. The Lord said to him, "Ananias."

He answered, "I'm here, Lord."

The Lord said to him, "Get up and go to the street called Straight Street, and ask at the house of Judas for a man called Saul. Saul is now praying to Me, and he's seen you in a vision coming to him and putting your hand on him, so he can get his sight back."

Ananias said, "Lord, I've heard lots of people talking about this man, about the terrible things he's done to Your people in Jerusalem. I know he's come here with letters from the chief priests, giving him power to arrest everyone who calls on You to be saved."

But Jesus said, "I want you to go to see him, because I've chosen him to preach My gospel to the Gentiles, and to kings, and to the children of Israel. And I will show him what great sufferings he must bear for My sake."

Then Ananias obeyed and went to the house of Judas. Putting his hands on Saul, he said, "Brother Saul, the Lord Jesus, who appeared to you as you were coming to Damascus, has sent me to put my hands on you, that you can receive your sight and be filled with the Holy Spirit."

Immediately Saul's eyes were healed and he could see, and he stood up and was baptized. After he had eaten some food, his strength came back. He stayed with the believers who were in Damascus, and went into the synagogues and preached about Christ to the people, telling them that Jesus was the Son of God.

Everyone who heard Saul was amazed, and said, "Isn't this the man who persecuted the believers in Jerusalem, and came here to arrest the followers of Jesus and take them to the chief priests to be punished?"

Saul now becomes known as Paul, although both names are really the same. Saul is a Jewish name that he used in the past when he was a Pharisee. Paul is the Roman equivalent of Saul, and his father was a Roman. Paul/Saul soon saw his mission as being especially to tell the good news of Jesus to the Gentiles. So using the Roman name of Paul, would have helped him be accepted by them. So from here on we will call him by the name we all know — Paul. For a time, however, many Jews would have still thought of him as Saul.

Paul preached more and more powerfully, and in Damascus he showed the Jews that the Scriptures proved that Jesus was the promised Saviour. Although they wouldn't believe, they couldn't deny what Paul said. After some time, the Jews who refused to believe were so angry that they discussed with each other about finding some way to kill him.

They watched day and night, waiting to capture Paul when he went out through the gates of the city. But the believers heard about this plot and one night they lowered Paul in a large basket from a window that was over the city wall, so he escaped from Damascus and made his way to Jerusalem.

When Paul reached Jerusalem he went to the believers who were there, because now, instead of hating them, he loved them and wanted to be with them. But of course they were afraid of him, and wouldn't believe he had become a disciple of Jesus.

Barnabas, one of the men who had sold land and given the money to the poor, took Paul to the apostles and told them how Paul had seen Jesus on his journey, and how he had been preaching the good news of Jesus boldly in Damascus.

Then the apostles accepted Paul, and he stayed with them and preached in Jerusalem. But some of the Jews at Jerusalem, like those at Damascus, were determined to kill him. When the apostles heard about it, they sent Paul away to a city called Tarsus, which was in a country called Asia Minor, where Paul was born.

After this, the Bible says, the churches had peace: that is, no one troubled or persecuted the Christians. By "churches" are meant groups of believers meeting together — not the buildings or houses in which they met.

As Peter continued his journey through different parts of the land, visiting groups of believers on the way, he reached the city of Lydda. There he found a man called Aeneas, who was suffering from paralysis, and had been in bed for eight years.

Peter said to him, "Aeneas, Jesus Christ makes you well. Stand up, and make your bed."

Aeneas stood up immediately, and many of the people who lived at Lydda and in the country around it saw him after he was healed, and they believed in Jesus.

At Joppa, a city not far from Lydda, there was a disciple called Dorcas, who was also known as Tabitha. She was always doing good things to help the poor. Suddenly she fell sick and died. The people washed her body and made it ready for burial, laying it in an upstairs room. Because the city of Lydda was near Joppa, the believers heard that Peter was there. So they sent two men to ask him to hurry and come to them.

When they'd brought Peter to the house, they took him upstairs to where the body of Dorcas lay. All the poor widows she'd helped stood around Peter, showing the coats and clothes Dorcas had made for them while she was alive.

Then Peter put everyone out of the room, and kneeled down and prayed. Turning to the dead body, he said, "Dorcas, wake up!"

She woke up like someone who had been asleep, and when she saw Peter, she sat up. He reached out his hand and helped her stand. Then he called everyone who was in the house, and gave her to them.

Peter stayed many days in Joppa, at the house of a man called Simon, who was a tanner and leatherworker.

Acts 10-14

Peter baptizes Cornelius; the apostles in Jerusalem find fault with Peter; he tells them of his vision; he is set free from prison by an angel; Barnabas and Paul preach in several cities; Paul is attacked at Lystra and they return to Antioch.

THERE was a man in the city of Caesarea called Cornelius, who was a centurion in the Roman army. He wasn't a Jew, but he was a good man who believed in God and taught his family to believe in God. He gave generously to the poor, and always prayed to the one true God. At about three in the afternoon (the ninth hour) Cornelius had a vision. In it, an angel came to him and said, "Cornelius."

When Cornelius saw the angel he was afraid, and said, "What do you want, sir?"

The angel said, "God has heard your prayers, and seen the help you've given to the poor. Now send some men to Joppa to find a man called Peter. He's staying in the house of Simon, a tanner, by the sea. When he comes here, he'll tell you what to do."

After the angel had gone, Cornelius called two of his servants who waited on him, and also a soldier who believed in God, whom he kept with him all the time. When he'd told them what the angel said, he explained they had to go to Joppa.

The next day they went on their journey and came near the city. Peter, who didn't know they were coming, went up on the rooftop to pray. Many of the houses in which the people lived had flat roofs, and often a small room was built on top where anyone of the family could go and be alone, and pray to God.

Peter went up there to pray about midday (the sixth hour). As he prayed, he felt hungry and wanted to eat. Then he had a dream, or vision. He saw the sky above him open, and something like a huge sheet, held up at the four corners, was let down to the ground in front of him. In this sheet he could see all kinds of wild animals, including reptiles and birds.

Then a voice said, "Get up, Peter. Kill and eat."

The Book of Exodus tells how Moses commanded the Children of Israel not to eat any of the animals that were called unclean. Peter could see some of these animals in the sheet. So when the voice told him to kill and eat them, he said, "I can't do it, Lord. I've never eaten anything that's forbidden or unclean."

Then the voice said, "What God has made clean, don't call forbidden or unclean."

These words were spoken three times, and then the sheet was lifted back to heaven.

It was God who sent the vision to Peter, and the reason He sent it was this: The Jews who had become Christians thought that because God had chosen them long ago for His people, they must be better than the people of other nations (the Gentiles), so Jesus came to save only them. They called other nations unclean, and some of the new Christians were refusing to preach the good news of Jesus to the Gentiles. But now God was teaching Peter that this was wrong. The animals he'd seen in the vision represented those other nations, and God intended to show Peter that he mustn't call them unclean any longer. He mustn't refuse to teach them, but preach to them just as he preached to the Jews, because God had made those nations as well as the Jews, and had sent Jesus to save them also.

While Peter was wondering what the vision could mean, the servants of Cornelius came to Simon's house and stood inside the gate and asked if Peter was there. Then the Holy Spirit spoke to Peter, and said, "Three men are looking for you. Get up and go with them without being afraid, for I have sent them."

Peter went down to the men, and said to them, "I'm the person you're looking for. Why are you here?"

They said, "Cornelius, the centurion, who's a good man and someone who worships God, and is well thought of by all the Jews, was told by a holy angel to send for you to come to his house. He wants to hear what you have to say."

Then Peter invited the men into Simon's house, and they stayed there that night. The next morning Peter travelled with them to Caesarea, and some of the believers who lived in Joppa went with them.

The next day they came to Caesarea. Cornelius was expecting them, and had already invited his relations and close friends to be with him when Peter came. As Peter entered his house, Cornelius fell down and worshipped him. But Peter said, "Stand up. I'm only a man like yourself!"

Peter went in with Cornelius and found people who, like Cornelius, were not Jews but Gentiles. Peter said to them, "You know that the Jews say it's wrong to make friends with people from other nations, because the Jews think themselves better, and call people from other countries common and unclean. But God has used a vision to teach me not to call these people common or unclean. So I came here as soon as you sent for me. So please tell me why you wanted me to come."

Cornelius said, "Four days ago I was fasting and praying in my house, and an angel stood in front of me in bright clothing, and said, "Cornelius, God has heard your prayers, and seen how you help the poor. Send to Joppa for a man called Peter. He's staying in the house of Simon, a tanner, by the sea. When he comes, he'll tell how you and all your family can be saved. So I sent for you immediately, and you have kindly come. Now we're all here together to hear what God has told you to say to us."

Then Peter said, "I can truthfully say now that God doesn't choose one nation to be His people more than another. But in every nation He takes for His children those people who worship Him, and do what's right. You've heard what's being preached to the Children of Israel about Jesus: how God sent Him into the world, and how He went about doing good and healing people who were possessed by demons, for God was with him. Yet the Jews took Him and put Him to death. But God raised Him up again on the third day, and showed Him to us, His apostles, who ate and drank with Him after He had risen. And He sent us to preach to everyone, and tell them that God has appointed Him to be the judge of the living and the dead. For He is the One the prophets were writing about when they said that everyone who believes in Him will have their sins forgiven."

While Peter was still speaking, the Holy Spirit came on Cornelius and on the other Gentiles who were with him. The Jews who had come with Peter from Joppa were astonished, because before that time they thought that God didn't care for the Gentiles. Now they could see that He had sent His Holy Spirit on them. They heard the Gentiles speaking in other languages which they had never understood before, through the power of the Holy Spirit.

Then Peter said, "Surely these men should be baptized,

because the Holy Spirit has been sent to them as well as to us." And he told them to be baptized in the name of Jesus the Messiah. Then Cornelius pleaded with him to stay with them for a few days.

It wasn't long before the apostles and disciples at Jerusalem heard that Peter had visited Cornelius and his Gentile friends in Caesarea. So when Peter returned to Jerusalem they quarrelled with him, and said, "You went to a house to visit men who are Gentiles, *and* you ate with them!"

So Peter told them everything that had happened to him: how God had taught him through the vision that he was to preach the good news of Jesus to the Gentiles also, and had told him to go with the men Cornelius sent.

"And," Peter said, "while I was preaching to Cornelius and his friends, the Holy Spirit came on them, just as He did on us who are Jews at the day of Pentecost. Therefore, as God sent His Spirit on them, who was I to go against Him?"

When the apostles and disciples heard this, they stopped criticising Peter, and gave thanks, saying, "Then God has given new hearts to the Gentile, so they can be saved as well as us."

When Stephen was put to death, some of the followers of Jesus fled from Jerusalem to the city of Antioch, in the land of Syria. When they got there they preached to the Gentiles. God helped them, so a large number of people became followers of Jesus.

When news of this reached Jerusalem, the apostles sent Barnabas to Antioch to see exactly what was happening there. When Barnabas saw how many people believed, he was glad, and encouraged them to go on in their new life by serving the Lord faithfully. Barnabas was a good man, whose heart was full of the Holy Spirit and faith; and through his preaching about the good news of Jesus, many more people believed in Jesus and became His followers.

Then Barnabas went to Tarsus to look for Paul, and when he found him he took him back to Antioch. They stayed for a whole year with the church in Antioch, with the believers who met together, explaining the good news of Jesus to many people. It was in Antioch that the believers were first called Christians, the name still used today.

Some men who were prophets came to Antioch from Jerusalem. One of them was called Agabus. He announced that a great famine was coming in all lands. Then the Christians at Antioch determined to send help to the persecuted believers in Jerusalem, and they sent money to them by Barnabas and Paul, each Christian giving as much as they were able.

About that time, Herod Agrippa, (not Herod the Great from the birth of Jesus, but Herod who had John the Baptist beheaded), began to persecute the Christians. He killed James, one of the apostles, with the sword. Then, because he saw it pleased the Jews, he took Peter and put him in prison, putting a guard of soldiers to watch over him night and day, to make sure he couldn't escape. Herod intended to bring Peter out of prison after the Passover and show him to the people, and then put him to death.

Peter was kept in prison, but the church in Jerusalem were praying for him every day. On the night before he was to be brought out to Herod to be executed, Peter was sleeping between two soldiers, secured with two chains that were fastened to the soldiers' hands, so if he moved they would know it.

An angel came to Peter, and a light shone in the prison.

The angel touched Peter's side and woke him, and said, "Get up quickly!"

The soldiers stayed asleep, and the chains fell from Peter's hands, and the angel said to him, "Get dressed, put on your sandals, and follow me."

Peter followed him, but he thought it was only a dream, or a vision. When they went past the guard of soldiers, they came to the iron gate that led into the city, and the gate opened of its own accord. So they went out and walked on through the first street, where the angel left Peter.

When he had time to think about what had happened, he said to himself, "Now I know for certain that the Lord has sent His angel to save me from Herod and from the Jews, who expected to kill me."

He went to the house of Mary, the mother of the disciple whose name was John Mark, where many Christians were gathered together praying. As Peter knocked at the door, a young woman called Rhoda came to see who it was. When she heard Peter's voice calling through the door, she was so excited that she forgot to open the door for him, and ran back and told everyone in the house that Peter was there.

They said to her, "You're mad. Peter is in prison!" (It is worth wondering why the Christians were praying, if they didn't expect an answer to the prayers!)

Rhoda insisted it was Peter at the door. Then they said, "Then it must be his spirit."

Peter kept on knocking, and when they opened the door and saw him they were dumbfounded. He signalled with his hand for them to be quiet, told them how the Lord had rescued him from prison. He said, "Go and tell the other apostles what's happened." Then he left them, and went to another place.

As soon as it was morning, the soldiers wondered where

Peter had gone, for they'd seen nothing of what had happened. When Herod Agrippa questioned them, he found they had no idea what had become of Peter, so he ordered them put to death.

After this, there was a special day when Herod dressed in his royal robes, sat on his throne and made a speech to the people. As they heard him, they shouted out, "It's the voice of a god, not a man!"

Herod was filled with pride when he heard them, because he liked the idea of people worshipping him as if he were a god. But the Lord God was angry with him, and a dreadful disease struck Herod down. His insides were eaten by maggots until he died.

Barnabas and Paul brought the money which had been sent by the Christians at Antioch, and gave it to the poor Christians in Jerusalem. Afterwards they returned to Antioch, taking with them the disciple whose name was John Mark.

In Antioch, there were other Christian preachers and teachers beside Barnabas and Paul. While they were worshipping the Lord, the Holy Spirit spoke to them and told them to send Barnabas and Paul away from Antioch to other countries, to preach the good news of Jesus to the people who lived there. So after they had all fasted and prayed together, the Christians laid their hands on the heads of Barnabas and Paul, and sent them away.

They sailed in a ship to the island of Cyprus. In the main city of the island, called Salamis, they went to the synagogue and taught the Jews. There were Jews living not only in the land of Judea, but in all the countries around that area. Wherever they lived, they built synagogues to worship in. At this time, John Mark was with Paul and Barnabas. They had not brought John Mark to preach, but to help them in other ways while they were on their journey.

They came to another city in the island of Cyprus, called Paphos. There they found a Jew called Elymas who was a false prophet. He was with the governor of the country. The governor was a wise man, and he sent for Barnabas and Paul to come and explain the good news of Jesus to him. But Elymas spoke against them, and tried to keep the governor from believing what they taught.

Paul looked at Elymas, and said, "You are full of lies and all kinds of evil trickery, you child of the devil. Are you never going to stop speaking evil about the things the Lord has told us to teach? And now, the Lord is going to punish you. You will be blind for a time, not even able to see the sun."

Immediately Elymas groped about like a person in the dark, looking for someone to lead him by the hand. Then the governor, when he saw the miracle that Paul had done, believed what the apostle said.

John Mark, Paul and Barnabas sailed from Paphos, and came to the city of Perga, in the country called Asia Minor. There John Mark left Paul and Barnabas, and returned to Jerusalem, because he was unwilling to go with them and help them any further on their journey.

So Paul and Barnabas went on to the city of Antioch. This wasn't the Antioch from which they first set out, but another city of the same name in Asia Minor. On the Sabbath day they went to the synagogue and sat down. After the Scriptures had been read, as they were every Sabbath, the rulers of the synagogue said to Paul and Barnabas. "Brothers, if you have any words to say to the people, please speak them now."

Then Paul stood up and said, "Men of Israel and everyone here who fears God, listen to me. The God of the Children of Israel chose our fathers to be His people, and by His mighty power set them free when they were living as strangers in the land of Egypt. Afterwards He took care of them for about forty years while they wandered in the desert. And when He had destroyed the evil nations of Canaan, He divided that land among them by lot. He gave them judges to rule over them for about four hundred and fifty years, until the time of Samuel, the prophet. Then the people asked for a king, and God gave them Saul. Then, when God had taken Saul away, He made David king.

"And now," Paul said, "as He promised, God has sent Jesus to you. Jesus was descended from David. But the people of Jerusalem and their rulers, because they didn't know Him, put Him to death. But God raised Him from the dead, and He was seen for many days after He had risen. He was seen by His apostles, who are sent out to tell the people about Him. And so we have come here to tell you the good news, that Jesus is the Saviour, the Messiah who was promised, and He will forgive all your sins if you will believe and trust in Him. So be careful, now you've been told about Him, that you don't refuse to believe, and so at last perish."

As Paul and Barnabas were leaving the synagogue, the people asked them to come back on the next Sabbath day and tell them more.

On the next Sabbath it seemed as though the whole city came to hear them. But when the Jews saw such a crowd coming they were not at all pleased, and spoke against the things Paul was saying, contradicting them and blaspheming.

So Paul and Barnabas spoke boldly to the Jews, and said, "It was right for us to preach the good news to you first, but since you won't hear it, and don't care to be saved, we will now preach it to the Gentiles. This is what God has told us to do. He said Jesus would be a Saviour, not just to the Jews, but to all the nations on earth."

When the Gentiles heard this they were glad. But the Jews stirred up the chief men and the rulers, and raised an angry mob against Paul and Barnabas, until they were driven out of Antioch.

They went next to the city of Iconium. At Iconium they went to the synagogue and taught the people about Jesus, and God gave them power to do miracles, so that many people, both Jews and Gentiles, believed. But in this city, as in Antioch, the Jews who refused to believe stirred up the people until they were ready to stone the apostles.

Realising what was happening, Paul and Barnabas fled to another city, called Lystra, and preached there.

In Lystra there was a man who'd been so lame since birth that he'd never been able to walk. He was sitting near the place where Paul was preaching, and heard him. Paul could see that the man had faith, and believed Jesus could make him well. So Paul called out loudly, "Stand up on your feet!"

And the man leaped up and walked.

When the people of Lystra saw the miracle, they shouted out in their own language, "These men are gods who've come down to us from heaven looking like men."

Then they called Barnabas Jupiter, and they called Paul Mercury, which were the names of their gods. Then the priests from the Temple of Jupiter brought oxen covered with wreaths of flowers, intending to sacrifice them to the apostles, in the way they sacrificed them to their gods.

When Barnabas and Paul saw it, they ripped their clothes to show their disapproval, and ran to the people, calling out, "Why are you doing this? We are men just like you. We've come to preach to you, and persuade you to worship only the true God who made heaven and earth, and the sea, and everything in them."

Even so, the apostles could hardly stop the people from offering up sacrifices to them. But some of the Jews who had driven them out of Antioch and Iconium, came to Lystra, and told the people that Barnabas and Paul were wicked men, and were trying to deceive them all.

Then immediately the people of Lystra, who not long before had wanted to worship the apostles, tried to kill them. They threw stones at Paul and dragged him out of the city, thinking he was dead. But while the believers were standing around him, he got to his feet and returned to the city.

The next day Paul went with Barnabas to another city, called Derbe. When they'd preached the good news of Jesus there, they returned to all the cities where the people had persecuted them. They spoke to the new Christians who lived in those cities, persuading them to keep on believing in the Lord Jesus, and explaining that they must accept trouble and sorrow if they wanted to serve God, and be among those who entered into His kingdom.

On their way back to Antioch, Paul and Barnabas put men, called elders, in charge of the churches in the cities they passed through. Eventually they arrived back in Antioch where they'd started their journey. There they called all the Christians together and told them how they'd preached the good news of Jesus to the Gentiles, as well as to the Jews, in the places where they'd been. And they stayed a long time with the believers in Antioch.

Acts 15-18

Some men tell the disciples they must keep the law of Moses; the apostles meet together to decide this question; Paul and Barnabas part company; Paul and Silas visit Lystra; they are put in prison; the jailer is converted; Paul preaches in Athens and visits Corinth.

SOME MEN came from Jerusalem to Antioch and told the disciples they couldn't be saved unless they obeyed all the Law of Moses and kept many other Jewish customs.

So Paul and Barnabas talked with these men, and asked them why they were putting God to the test by placing a yoke on the neck of the disciples that neither their fathers nor they had been able to bear. They meant that people were being weighed down with all the things they were told they had to do to please God.

However, when Paul and Barnabas came to Jerusalem, they were welcomed by the believers, and they told them everything that God had done with them.

After listening to a long argument about keeping the Jewish laws and customs, Peter said to the men who wanted even Gentile Christians to obey the Old Testament laws, "God, who knows the heart, has given the Gentiles the Holy Spirit just as He did to us. He has not made any division between us and them, and has made their hearts clean by faith. So why are you putting God to the test and unsettling their minds by placing a burden on the Gentile believers? We believe we're saved through the grace of the Lord Jesus, not by keeping lots of rules and regulations, and that is how they will be saved, too."

Then James said, "We should not trouble the faith of the Gentiles who turn to God by giving them lots of rules and regulations to keep, although we must encourage them to live godly lives."

The apostles and elders chose two men, Judas and Silas, to return to Antioch with Paul and Barnabas. They wrote a letter for them to take with them, to give to the Christians in Antioch, and other cities, telling them they were free from the Law of Moses, and that what God wanted them to do now was to obey the words of Jesus which said they should repent of their sins and believe in Him; and love God in their hearts and live clean, godly lives.

When the Gentiles in the different churches read it, they rejoiced because they found it so encouraging.

One day Paul said to Barnabas, "Let's go and visit our fellow Christians in all the cities where we preached the gospel, and see how they're getting on."

Barnabas was willing to go, and he wanted to take John Mark with him; but Paul thought it best not to take John Mark, who, when they took him before, left them, and was unwilling to stay with them to the end of their journey. So they disagreed about this matter, and their disagreement was so great that they parted company.

Then Barnabas took John Mark and sailed to the island of Cyprus, but Paul chose Silas and went to Syria, visiting the young churches there.

When Paul came to Lystra, the city where he had healed the lame man, he found a young man called Timothy whose mother was a Jew, and a disciple of Jesus, and his father was a Gentile. Timothy was well spoken of by the Christians at Lystra. Ever since he was a small child he'd been taught to know what was in the Scriptures (the Old Testament), and to obey the Lord. When Paul saw how wise and good a young man Timothy was, he chose him to go with him and Silas, so Timothy could learn to preach the good news of Jesus.

They came to Troas, a city near the sea. One night, Paul had a vision. He saw a man standing in front of him, who said, "Come over to Macedonia and help us."

Macedonia was a country across the sea; so Paul, and those who were with him, sailed in a ship from Troas and reached a city of Macedonia called Philippi, which was a Roman colony.

On the Sabbath day they went a short way out of the city, to a place by the side of a river where the Jews used to meet together to pray. They sat down and talked with the women who came there.

A woman called Lydia, who was a seller of purple cloth, heard them speaking. Then the Lord sent His Spirit into her heart, so she listened carefully to what Paul said, and she believed and trusted in Jesus. When she and her whole family had been baptized, she begged Paul and his friends, "If you think me a true Christian, come and stay at my house."

So they went with her to her home.

There was a young woman in Philippi who had an evil spirit, and she earned money for her owners by claiming she could tell people what would happen to them in the future. She followed Paul and his companions, and kept calling out, "These men are the servants of God, and they show us the way to be saved."

This she did for many days. It is unlikely that she was doing this to help Paul and his companions, but wanted to disturb the crowd and disrupt what Paul was preaching. So Paul, being irritated that she followed them, turned and said to the evil spirit, "I command you, in the name of Jesus Christ, to come out of her." And the spirit came out of her.

When the owners of the young woman saw that she was now well, and could no longer earn money for them by repeating what the evil spirit said, they were angry, and caught Paul, Silas and Timothy, and dragged them before the rulers. They said, "These men, who are Jews, are causing great trouble in our city, by teaching the people things which aren't right for them to do."

Then the people of Philippi shouted out in protest against Paul and Silas, and the rulers ordered them to be beaten. After they had beaten them, they put them in prison, telling the jailer to keep them securely locked up. So the jailor took them into the inner prison and made their feet fast in the stocks, heavy pieces of wood, so they couldn't escape.

In the middle of the night Paul and Silas prayed and sang praises to God, and the other prisoners heard them. Suddenly there was an earthquake which shook the prison, and immediately all the doors opened by themselves, and the chains that secured the prisoners fell off them.

The keeper of the prison, waking up and seeing the prison doors open, was afraid he would be put to death for allowing the prisoners to escape. So he drew his sword and was about to kill himself, thinking the prisoners had all got away. But Paul called out to him loudly, "Don't harm yourself. We are all still here."

Then the jailer called for a light and came trembling into the dungeon where Paul and Silas were. Kneeling down, he said, "Men, what must I do to be saved?"

They said, "Believe in the Lord Jesus Christ, and you will be saved."

Then they told him, and all who were in his house, about the Saviour, and explained the good news of Jesus to them. And they believed, and were all baptized. Then the jailer took Paul and Silas and washed the wounds from their beating. He also brought food and gave it to them to eat. And the jailer was so happy, because he and his family were now Christians, and knew their sins were forgiven.

In the morning, the rulers sent some officers to the prison who said to the jailer, "Let those men go."

So the jailer said to Paul, "The rulers have sent word that I am to let you go."

The Jews were servants to the Romans, but Paul's father, although he was a Pharisee, a strict Jew, had been made free. The New Testament writers don't say whether he bought his freedom for money, or received it as a reward from the Emperor for doing something that pleased him. So because Paul's father was made a free Roman, Paul was automatically one too. And it was against the law to beat a free Roman.

When the rulers sent officers to say he could go, Paul said, "They've taken us, who are both Romans, and although no crime has been proved against us, they've beaten us in front of all the people. So if they want us to go, let the rulers come and take us out, so the people will know we were unjustly beaten and thrown into prison."

When the rulers heard that Paul say he was a Roman they were afraid in case they might be in serious trouble for what they'd done. So they came and begged Paul to leave the city. Then he and Silas left the prison and went to the house of Lydia. After meeting there with the other Christians, and talking with them to comfort them, they left Philippi and continued their journey, taking Timothy with them.

They came to another city of Macedonia, called Thessalonica, where there was a synagogue. Paul went into it and preached to the Jews for three Sabbath days. As he did in every city, he explained the Scriptures to them, showing from what the prophets had written, that Jesus was the Messiah, the Saviour. Then some of the Jews believed, and so did many of the Gentiles.

But the Jews who refused to believe became angry when they saw others believing. So they took some troublemakers with them and made a disturbance in the city, and went to the house where Paul and Silas stayed to bring them out to face the people. When they couldn't find them there, they caught the owner of the house, whose name was Jason, and took him to the rulers.

They said, "The men called Christians, who've been making such trouble and misunderstanding in other places, have now come here. They disobey the decrees of Caesar, and say there's another king, called Jesus. And now Jason has let these men stay in his house."

Then the rulers made Jason promise that Paul and Silas would cause no more disturbance in the city, and then they let him go. But the men who were Christians in Thessalonica knew it wasn't safe for Paul and Silas to stay there any longer, so they sent them away at night to a city called Berea.

When Paul, Silas and Timothy reached Berea, they went to the synagogue to preach to the Jews. The Jews in Berea were more willing to learn than those in Thessalonica, for they listened to the good news of Jesus, and after hearing it, they read every day in the Scriptures to see whether the things that Paul and Silas told them out of the prophets were true. Many of the Jews believed, and so did the Gentiles, both men and women.

When the Jews who had driven Paul away from Thessalonica heard he was preaching in Berea, they came there to stir up the people against him. Then the Christians in Berea sent Paul away, but Silas and Timothy stayed.

The men who went with Paul took him to Athens, which was the chief city of Greece. The people of Athens were considered the wisest people living at that time, and were famous for their learning; yet they worshipped false gods.

They made beautiful statues of these gods, and built splendid temples and altars to them in different parts of their city. Among the altars was one with these words on it: TO THE UNKNOWN GOD. Although they had many gods, the people of Athens believed there was one God they had never learned about, so they built this altar to Him.

As Paul walked through the streets of Athens he could see the city was full of idols. This upset him, and he preached not only to the Jews in their synagogue, but he went every day to the market place where the people of the city met. Here he explained the good news of Jesus to them.

When the philosophers, or wise men of Athens, heard him, some of them asked, "What is this man is talking about?" Others told them, "He seems to be telling about some new and strange gods." They said this, because Paul preached about Jesus and the resurrection.

They took Paul to the place where the chief court of Athens met on Mars Hill in the centre of the city, and said to him, "Tell us now what this gospel, this good news, is that you're preaching. You speak strange words, and we'd like to know what they mean."

The people of Athens spent their time either telling or hearing about some new thing. So Paul stood up, and said, "Men of Athens, I can see you think a great deal about the gods you worship. As I walked through your city, looking at your temples, your altars, and your images, I saw an altar with these words written on it: TO THE UNKNOWN GOD. I now want to tell you about that God you worship, even though you don't know Him."

Then Paul told them that God, who made the world, and made them, didn't live in temples such as they built, neither was He like the idols of gold, and silver and stone which people made. Paul told his listeners that while they knew no better than to worship such idols, God hadn't destroyed them for doing it, but had allowed them to live, and had given them food and clothing and everything they needed. But now, Paul said, God wanted them to stop their worship of idols, telling them to repent of their sins and believe in Jesus, because God had appointed a day when He would send Jesus to judge them. Paul explained that God had given them a proof that He would do this, by raising Jesus up from the dead.

When the men of Athens heard Paul speak of the resurrection, or the rising up from the dead, some of them refused to listen anymore and made fun of him, but others said, "We'd like to hear you speak again about this."

A number of those who had heard him, believed. Among them was Dionysius, one of the members of the chief court of Athens, and a woman called Damaris, and others with them.

After a time, Paul left Athens and travelled to the city of Corinth where he found a Jew called Aquila, with his wife Priscilla. They had recently come from Italy, having been expelled as a result of Claudius Caesar's order to expel all Jews from Rome.

The Jews always taught their sons some business or trade while they were young, so when they were older they would be able to support themselves. While he was young, Paul had been taught to be a tent maker. Even though he was now an apostle, whenever he needed money, he made tents for his living rather than relying on friends to support him.

Because Aquila was also a tent maker, Paul went to stay and work with him. Every Sabbath day he went to the synagogue and taught the people, persuading both the Jews and the Gentiles to believe and trust in Jesus the Saviour. When some of the Jews said terrible things about Jesus, Paul told them, "I've done my duty in telling you about Jesus. If you don't want to be saved, the fault is yours. From now on, I'm going to preach to the Gentiles."

Corinth, like Athens, was a large city, but the people who lived there were immoral. One night the Lord spoke to Paul in a vision, and told him that many of the people in Corinth would become Christians. Then He told Paul to preach boldly and without fear; "Because," the Lord said, "I am with you to take care of you, and no one will hurt you."

Paul stayed in Corinth for eighteen months, preaching to the people. But the Jews in Corinth who wouldn't believe, rioted against Paul and brought him to the governor, and said, "This man teaches men to worship God in a way that's wrong."

When Paul was going to answer them, the governor said to those who brought him, "If this man has done something that's really wrong, I ought to hear what you have to say against him. But if it's only a question about your Jewish worship, you can see to it yourselves. I won't be a judge between you in such matters." Then the governor sent them away.

The Gentiles were angry at the Jews for persecuting Paul, and caught hold of the chief ruler of the synagogue and beat him in front of the governor. But the governor didn't stop them, because he cared nothing about the beliefs and customs of the Jews.

Acts 19-23

Some Jews attempt to cast out evil spirits; Demetrius stirs up the silversmiths; Paul preaches at Troas; raises Eutychus from the dead; sends for the church elders at Ephesus; visits Tyre and Caesarea; Agabus predicts Paul being taken prisoner; Paul is taken prisoner at the Temple in Jerusalem and sent to Caesarea.

AFTER Paul had stayed in Corinth for a long time, he said goodbye to the Christians there, and sailed east to Syria where he came to the city of Ephesus. He was in Ephesus for three years preaching the good news of Jesus, until everyone in that part of Asia, both Jews and Gentiles, had heard it.

One day, Paul found a group of about twelve believers, and asked them, "Did you receive the Holy Spirit when you believed?"

They said, "No, we haven't heard that there is a Holy Spirit."

So Paul asked them, "What baptism did you receive?"

They said, "We received John's baptism."

They were saying that they had been baptized in the way John the Baptist baptized people many years earlier, and Paul knew they could now receive the Holy Spirit inside them, because Jesus had risen from the dead.

He told them, "John's baptism was a baptism of repentance. But," he said, "John told the people to believe in the Messiah coming after him, that is, to believe in Jesus."

When they heard this, they were baptized in the name of

the Lord Jesus, and when Paul placed his hands on them, the Holy Spirit came on them, and they spoke in other languages, and prophesied.

God gave Paul power to do wonderful miracles, so that handkerchiefs and clothing he had used, when given to people who were sick or had evil spirits, made them well.

Then some Jews who spent their time wandering about from one place to another, claimed they could also cast out evil spirits. They spoke to the evil spirits in the way Paul did, saying, "We command you, in the name of Jesus whom Paul talks about, to come out."

There were seven brothers who did this on one occasion, but the evil spirit said, "Jesus I know, and Paul I know; but who are you?"

The man in whom the evil spirit was, leaped on them and beat them so badly that they ran out of the house wounded, with their clothes torn. Everybody heard about it, and many who had led sinful lives, believed, and came to Paul confessing the wrong they had done. Others who before that time had tricked the people by claiming they could work real magic, brought the books which taught about such things, and burned them where all the people could see.

When they had counted up the cost of the books, they found it to be 50,000 silver coins, one silver coin being a day's wage for a working man. Yet the owners of these books wanted to destroy them, rather than continue using them to do what they knew would offend God, or sell them to get their money back.

The people of Ephesus worshipped an idol they claimed had fallen down from heaven. Its name was Artemis , and they had in their city a splendid temple where this idol was kept. Some people knew the god by the name of Diana. The temple was built from cedar and cypress wood, and marble and gold. The people took 220 years to build it. It was famous among all nations, and people from far and wide came to visit it because it was thought to be one of the most beautiful and wonderful buildings in the world.

There were men at Ephesus who made small copies of this temple out of silver, with an image of Artemis inside. These were called shrines. The silversmiths who made these shrines sold them to the local people and visitors, and in this way earned a lot of money. One of these men was called Demetrius. When he heard Paul telling the people to stop worshipping idols, he noticed many of them were obeying what Paul said.

So Demetrius called together all the workers who made silver shrines for Artemis, and said to them, "You know we get our wealth from making these shrines. You've heard that both here in Ephesus, and in almost every other city in Asia, this man Paul has been telling people that gods made by men's hands are false gods. So here's the problem. Not only will be unable to sell our shrines, but the great goddess Artemis won't be worshipped any longer because people will stop coming to her beautiful temple.

When the silversmiths heard what Demetrius said, they were furious, and shouted out, "Great is Artemis of the Ephesians."

The whole city was soon in chaos. Then the silver workers caught Gaius and Aristarchus, two Macedonian Christians who had come with Paul to Ephesus, and they hurried them along to the theatre (or stadium). When Paul wanted to go in and speak with them, the believers wouldn't let him, afraid he'd be injured. Some of the chief men of the city, who were Paul's friends, sent him a warning not to go, because the people were so worked up. Some of them were shouting one thing and some another, but they were all angry.

Many of the crowd who followed the workers into the theatre had no idea why they were there. The Jews also came there to say things against Paul. One of them, called Alexander, stood up and signalled with his hand for the people to be quiet and listen to what he had to say. When the people realized Alexander was a Jew, the noise continued, and the whole crowd kept shouting for about two hours, "Great is Artemis of the Ephesians!"

Then one of the chief officers of the city, called the city clerk, came into the theatre. As soon as the people were quiet, he said to them, "Men of Ephesus, who is there among you who doesn't know that the people of our city are worshippers of the great goddess Artemis, and of her image that fell down from heaven? Now as no one denies this, you ought to be careful, and do nothing in anger. You've brought the men called Christians here, but they've not robbed your temple, or spoken evil of your goddess.

"Now, if Demetrius, and any of the craft workers who are with him, have any complaint to make against the Christians, let that person go before the court and prove what wrong they've done. For we're in danger of being blamed by our rulers for this disturbance, because we can give no reason for it."

When the city clerk had said this, he sent the people away. After they'd gone, Paul called the believers to him, and bidding them farewell, he left them and returned to Macedonia.

When Paul had preached in the different cities of Macedonia, he returned to Troas, in Asia. On the first day of the week (Sunday), when the Christians came together to eat the bread and drink the wine as Jesus had told them at the Last Supper, Paul taught them, because he was leaving Troas the next day. The upstairs room where they met together was lit by many oil lamps, and Paul continued speaking until the middle of the night.

A young man called Eutychus was sitting in the upstairs window, listening to Paul. While Paul was speaking, Eutychus dropped off to sleep and fell out of the window and was killed. Paul went down to him, and putting his arms around him, said to everyone who stood by, "Don't be troubled. He's come to life again."

The young man's friends, when they saw he was alive, took him up and were thankful. When Paul returned upstairs and had eaten with the other believers, he carried on talking with them until it was morning. Then he left Troas.

Paul and some Christian believers who were with him sailed to the city of Miletus, which wasn't far from Ephesus. Because Paul had no time spare to go to Ephesus, he sent for the elders of the church there, to come and meet him. Paul was in a hurry to get to Jerusalem in time for the Feast of Pentecost.

When the Ephesian elders came, he said to them, "From the first day I came here to see you, and for the three years I stayed with you, you know how I lived all the time. I've been serving the Lord with humility, yet there have been many sorrows and trials because some of the Jews were always looking to harm me. And you know how when I preached to you, I didn't keep back anything you needed to hear, even if it was something that might offend you. I taught you in the synagogue and in your own houses, telling both the Jews and the Gentiles that they should repent of their sins and believe and trust in the Lord Jesus Christ.

"And now I'm going to Jerusalem. I don't know what will happen to me there, except that in every city I visit the Holy Spirit tells me that prison chains and troubles are waiting for me. Yet none of these things makes me afraid, nor do I care even if I'm put to death. I want to die with joy and finish the work the Lord Jesus has given me, as His minister, to do. This time I know that all of you who've heard me preach the good news of Jesus so often, will not see me again. So before I go, I want you to agree that if any of you are lost at the Judgment day, it won't be my fault, because I've not neglected to tell you how you can be saved, as God sent me to tell you."

When Paul had finished speaking, he knelt down and prayed with them. All the believers wept and put their arms round his neck and kissed him, being especially sad because he'd said they would never see him again. Then they went with him to the ship in which he sailed away from Miletus.

Paul reached the city of Tyre, where the ship was to unload its cargo. Finding some believers there, he stayed with them for seven days. As he was about to leave them, they brought their wives and children to see Paul by the shore, where they knelt down together and prayed. When they'd all said goodbye, Paul and the Christians who travelled with him went on board the ship, and the believers in Tyre returned to their own homes.

Next, Paul came to the city of Caesarea, and went to the house of Philip, one of the seven men on whom the apostles had laid their hands soon after the resurrection of Jesus. Philip was the evangelist who preached the good news of Jesus to the Ethiopian official as he rode in his chariot going back from Jerusalem to Ethiopia, and earlier had told the

Samaritans about Jesus.

While Paul was in Philip's house, a prophet called Agabus came to visit. He took Paul's belt and tied his own hands and feet together with it, and said, "The Holy Spirit has told me that this is how the Jews in Jerusalem will tie the man who owns this belt, and will give him to the Gentiles to be punished."

When the believers who were with Paul heard this, they wept, and begged him not to go to Jerusalem in case something bad should happen to him. But Paul said to them, "Are you weeping to upset me and break my heart? I'm ready not only to be tied up, but also to die at Jerusalem — if they kill me for preaching about Jesus."

When they saw that Paul could not be persuaded to stay, they stopped begging him not to go, and said, "Let the will of the Lord be done."

Paul and his group of believers left Caesarea and went up to Jerusalem, where the Christians welcomed him. The next day he went to see James, one of the apostles, and all the elders of the church were there to meet him. Then Paul told them about the places where he'd been, and how God had helped him, so that by his preaching many Gentiles believed. When they heard this they rejoiced and thanked God for everything that had been done.

Paul went up to the Temple in Jerusalem. While he was there, some Jews from Asia saw him and caught hold of him, calling out to all the people, "Men of Israel, help us. This is the man who teaches the people everywhere not to obey the Law of Moses, or to worship here. Not only this, he's brought some Gentiles with him into the Temple, and they're forbidden to come into this holy place!" They had earlier seen Trophimus the Ephesian with Paul in the city, and they imagined Paul had brought him into the Temple.

Soon all the city began to riot. The people caught hold of Paul, dragging him away from the Temple, and immediately the gates leading into the courts of the Temple were shut. As the mob were about to kill Paul, someone told the commander of the Roman soldiers, who stayed in a barracks near the Temple to guard it and keep order there.

Then the commander, taking some of his soldiers with him, ran into the crowd. When they saw him coming, they stopped beating Paul. The commander took Paul from them and ordered him to be secured with two chains, before asking the crowd who Paul was and what he'd done.

Some of the crowd cried one thing, and some another, so no one could tell what they were complaining about. Then the commander ordered Paul to be taken to the barracks. When they came to the stairs leading up to the barracks, the soldiers had to carry Paul to keep the people from trying to pull him away. They were shouting out, "Kill him! Kill him!"

As the soldiers were about to shut Paul in the barracks, he said to the commander, "May I speak to you?"

Not long before this, an Egyptian tricked four thousand Jews by claiming he was a prophet. He persuaded them to follow him out into the desert as assassins, to fight the Romans, and many of them were killed there. When the commander saw the people so angry, he thought Paul must be that same man. So he asked him, "Aren't you that Egyptian who led men out into the desert?"

Paul said, "No, I'm a Jew who was born in Tarsus, which is a well-known city. Please, let me speak to the people."

When permission had been given, Paul stood on the steps where everyone could see him, and signalled to them to be quiet. As soon as there was silence he spoke to them in

Hebrew, which he knew the Jews would understand.

He said, "I too am a Jew. I was born in Tarsus, but brought up here in Jerusalem. This is where a scholarly Jew called Gamaliel taught me all the laws that Moses spoke to our fathers. I wanted everyone to obey those laws, just as you do today. I persecuted and wanted to put to death everyone who followed Jesus, arresting them and sending men and women to prison. The high priest and all the council of the Sanhedrim will tell you what I say is true. They gave me letters to the Jews in Damascus, with permission to arrest any Christians I found there, and bring back them to Jerusalem to be punished.

"As I went on my journey and came near Damascus, suddenly at midday a great light shone from heaven around me. I fell down to the ground, and heard a voice, saying, 'Saul, Saul, why are you persecuting Me?' I said, 'Who are You, Lord?' The voice said, "I am Jesus, the One you are persecuting.'

"The men who were with me saw the light and were afraid, but they couldn't understand the words that were spoken. And I said, 'Lord, what do You want me to do?' The Lord Jesus said to me, 'Get up and go to Damascus, and there you will be told what you must do.'

"When I couldn't see, because the brightness of that light had blinded me, I was led by the hand to Damascus. After three days a disciple there, called Ananias, who feared God and was well thought of by all the Jews, came and stood by me. He said, 'Brother Saul, receive your sight.' And immediately I could see him. Ananias said to me, 'God has allowed you to see Jesus and hear Him speak, so that you can go and preach to all nations about Him.'

"Three years after that, when I was in Jerusalem and was praying in the Temple, I saw Jesus again in a vision, and heard Him say, 'Hurry up. Leave Jerusalem quickly, for the Jews won't believe what you're telling them about Me. I'm sending you far away to preach to the Gentiles.'"

The crowd of Jews, to whom Paul was speaking, listened until he mentioned about preaching to the Gentiles. Then they shouted out loudly, "Kill him, for a man like this is not fit to live!"

As they said this, in their rage they threw off their outer clothing and threw dust in the air. The Roman commander ordered that Paul should be brought back to the barracks and beaten, to make him confess any wrong things he'd done.

But as the soldiers tied him with cords and prepared to beat him, Paul said to the officer who stood nearby, "Is it lawful for you to beat a man who is a free Roman, before any crime has been proved against him?"

When the officer heard this, he went and told the commander. He said, "Be careful what you do, because this man is a Roman."

Then the commander who was called Claudius Lysias, came and said to Paul, "Tell me, *are* you a Roman?"

He answered, "Yes."

The commander said, "I paid a large sum of money to be made a free Roman."

Paul said, "But I was born a citizen." He could say this because his father was a freeman.

Then the men who were about to beat Paul left him alone. And the commander, after he heard that Paul was a Roman, was afraid in case he might be in trouble for having tied Paul up.

The next day, when the Roman commander wanted to know what the Jews accused Paul of, he ordered the council of the Sanhedrim to meet together, and brought Paul down and stood him before them.

Paul, looking intently at them, said, "Men and brothers, I've only done those things that my conscience told me were correct, right up until this moment."

Then Ananias, the high priest, ordered the people who stood near Paul to hit him across the mouth. Paul said, "God will strike you, you hypocrite, for claiming to try me according to the law, and yet ordering me to be struck before I'm proved guilty. What you've done is against the law."

The Jews said to Paul, "Do you insult the high priest?"

Paul said, "I didn't know he was the high priest. I know it's written in the Scriptures that we must not speak evil of the one who rules over us."

Then Paul tried again to speak to the men in the lie council, but soon there was such a great uproar among them that the commander was afraid Paul would be torn to pieces, so he ordered the soldiers to get Paul away from them by force, and take him into the barracks for his own safety.

The next night, while Paul was kept a prisoner, the Lord Jesus came and stood by him, and said, "Paul, don't be afraid. You've spoken about Me to the people here in Jerusalem, and you will also speak about Me in the city of Rome."

In the morning some of the Jews met together, and made a solemn promise that they would neither eat bread, nor drink water, until they'd killed Paul. There were more than forty who made this promise. Then they went to the chief priests and elders, and said, "We've agreed with each other that we won't eat or drink until we've killed Paul. Now, tell the Roman commander to bring him down tomorrow before the council, as though you want to ask him some more questions. And while he's on the way, we'll lie in wait and then jump on him and kill him."

But the son of Paul's sister overheard what the Jews said, and he went to the barracks and told Paul. Then Paul called one of the officers to him, and said, "Take this young man to the commander, for he has something important to tell him."

So the soldier took Paul's nephew to the commander, and said, "Paul the prisoner begged me to bring this young man to you."

Then the commander took Paul's nephew by the hand, and led him to a place where they were alone and asked him, "What do you have to tell me?

The young man answered, "The Jews are going to ask you to take Paul down before the council tomorrow, pretending they want to ask him some more questions. But you mustn't do it, because more than forty men will be lying in ambush along the way, and they've made a promise that they won't eat or drink until they've killed him. Even now they're waiting, hoping you'll do as they ask."

As the commander let the young man go, he said, "Make sure you don't let anyone know you've told me this."

The Roman governor of Judea was called Felix. He didn't live at Jerusalem, but at the city of Caesarea which was on the Mediterranean coast about sixty miles from Jerusalem. When the commander heard that the Jews wanted to kill Paul, he made up his mind to send him to the governor. So he called two centurions, and said to them, "Get two hundred foot soldiers and seventy horsemen, and two hundred spearmen ready to go to Caesarea at nine o'clock tonight. And send some mounts for Paul and the men who are with him to ride on, so he'll be safe on his journey to see the governor of Judea."

Claudius Lysias, the commander, also wrote a letter to the governor, saying, "The man I'm sending to you was caught by the Jews, who were about to kill him. So I went with soldiers and took him from them, for I heard he was a Roman. Because I wanted to know what evil they accused him of, I brought him before their council, and found that he had not done anything for which he ought to be put to death. When I was told that the Jews were still determined to kill him, I sent him to you, and ordered the Jews who accused him to go and tell you what they have against him. Farewell."

Then the soldiers took Paul and took him by night to the town of Antipatris, which was on the way to Caesarea. There the foot soldiers left him and returned to the fortress at Jerusalem, but the horsemen took him the rest of the way to the governor at Caesarea.

There, they gave the governor the letter which the Roman commander had sent. After reading the letter the governor asked Paul in what part of the empire he was born. When Paul told him it was Cilicia, he said, "I'll hear what you have to say when the Jews who accuse you have come here to Caesarea." And he ordered Paul to be kept in prison until they came.

Acts 24-29

The Jews accuse Paul, who defends himself before Felix and Agrippa; he appeals to Caesar; is sent to Rome; he is shipwrecked on the way; at Rome Paul preaches the gospel; the traditional manner of his death.

AFTER five days, Ananias, the high priest, and some of the council came from Jerusalem to Caesarea. They brought with them a lawyer called Tertullus, to give evidence against Paul in front of the governor.

When Paul was brought out of the prison to be tried, Tertullus began to accuse him, saying, "We have found this fellow to be an evil man, who is stirring up trouble and disorder among the Jews all over the world. He is a chief one among those who believe in Jesus of Nazareth. He has also brought Gentiles into the Temple, who are not allowed to go there. We would have tried him according to our law, to see what his punishment should be, but Lysias, the commander of the garrison, came with soldiers and took him from us by force, ordering us to come before you and accuse him. Now we're here, ready to prove all the things we speak against him."

When Tertullus had finished, the Jews who were with him said that all Tertullus had said was true. Then Paul, after the governor had given him permission, said, "It was only twelve days ago that I went up to Jerusalem to worship, and they found me in the Temple. But I wasn't arguing with anyone, nor was I trying to stir up the people. They cannot prove the things they speak against me. But this I confess to you, that I worship God in a way that's different from them, although I believe everything that is written in their Scriptures. I expect the dead, both the bad and the good, to rise up at the last day, just as the Jews themselves say they will. And because I believe this, I'm trying all the time to do nothing that my conscience tells me is wrong, either to God or to man."

Paul continued, "After being away from Jerusalem for many years, I came back to bring money to the poor Jews there, and also an offering to God. Some Jews from Asia found me in the Temple, but I wasn't there with a crowd, not was I causing any disturbance. *Those* Jews are the ones who should be here to give evidence if they have anything against me. Or let these Jews who are here now say whether they found any wrongdoing in me when I was taken before the council in Jerusalem — unless they want to say it was wrong for me to preach about the dead rising up from the graves at the Judgment day."

Felix stopped the trial and said, "When commander Lysias comes here, I will decide what to do with you." He sent the Jews away, and ordered the commander to keep Paul in prison, but to let him see any friends who might come to visit him.

Drusilla, the wife of Felix, was a Jew. A few days after this, Felix sent for Paul to come and speak to him and Drusilla, and explain the good news of Jesus to them. Felix already understood something about the Christian faith, which was known by some as the Way. As Paul spoke to them, persuading them to obey God, and not listen to temptation, he told them how they must be judged by God at the last day.

Felix thought of his sins, and was so afraid that he trembled. Yet he didn't repent of those sins, but sent Paul back to prison, saying, "Leave me now, and at some other time when it's more convenient, I'll send for you again to tell me about these things."

Felix knew Paul had brought a large gift of money to the Christians in Jerusalem, and he probably hoped Paul would offer him money to let him go free. Because of that, he sent for Paul several times to talk with him. But after two years, when another governor, called Festus, came to take Felix's place, instead of letting Paul go, Felix left him in prison.

When Festus, the new governor, came to Caesarea, the Jews asked him to send Paul to Jerusalem to be tried. They still intended to have men hidden somewhere on the way who would kill him. However, Festus said, "Paul will stay in Caesarea, and those who wish to accuse him can come here and say what complaint they have against him."

When the accusers came, the governor ordered Paul to be brought out to face them, and the Jews stood and accused him of many things. But Paul answered for himself, and said, "I have done nothing wrong against the Jewish laws, against the Temple, or against Caesar."

Then Festus, because he wanted to please the Jews, said to Paul, "Are you willing to go to Jerusalem and be tried there for these things they accuse you of?"

It was a law that any Roman citizen who was going to be put to death could ask to be taken before Caesar, the Emperor, and the Emperor would say whether he should die or be allowed to live. The Emperor at this time was Nero, an evil man. When Festus asked Paul if he was willing to go to Jerusalem to be tried before the Jews, Paul knew they were determined to kill him. So he said, "Jerusalem isn't the place where I ought to be tried. I've done nothing wrong to the

Jews, as you very well know. I ask to be taken before Caesar."

Then Festus said, "Have you really asked to be taken before Caesar? All right, then to Caesar you will go." He meant that Paul would be taken to the city of Rome, where the Emperor Caesar lived.

Some days after this, Agrippa II, who was king over another part of Israel, came with his sister Bernice to visit Festus in Caesarea. Festus told him about Paul. He said, "There's a man here in prison, and the chief priests and Jewish elders have asked me to put him to death."

Herod Agrippa II was a Jew, and when the governor told him some of the Jews wanted to put Paul to death, he said, "I'd like to hear what the man has to say."

Festus told him, "You can hear him tomorrow."

The next day Agrippa came with Bernice, dressed in their royal robes, with military officers and important men of the city around them. Festus sent for Paul to be brought from the prison, and he came with chains still fastened to him. Then Festus told Agrippa this was the man the Jews wanted to kill.

Agrippa said to Paul, "You have permission to speak for yourself, and answer the things which the Jews say against you."

Paul stood up and told King Agrippa he was very glad to explain himself, because he was sure the king had learned all about the laws of the Jews, and would understand what he was now going to say.

Then Paul said, "The Jews know very well how I've lived, and what I've done, ever since I was a child. For I also am a Jew, and if they spoke the truth they would admit I used to be one of the strictest among them. I, too, thought I ought to do many things against Jesus of Nazareth. I shut many of

His disciples in prison, and when they were tried and put to death, I was one of those who spoke against them. I punished them in every synagogue, and did all I could to make them speak against their Saviour.

"Being so angry with these believers I even went to other cities to look for them. But as I was going to Damascus, when I came near the city, I saw in the middle of the day a light from heaven, brighter than the sun. It shone all around me and the men who were with me. We were so afraid we all fell to the ground."

Then Paul told Agrippa and Festus, and everyone who was listening to him, how Jesus spoke to him, and said He had come to make Paul a minister of the good news of Jesus, and send him to preach the good news to the Gentiles, so that they could repent and have their sins forgiven.

"When I heard His voice," Paul said, "I didn't disobey what the Lord told me to do, but I went and preached to the Jews at Damascus and at Jerusalem, and also to the Gentiles, telling them to repent and obey God. And because I did this, the Jews caught me in the Temple and were about to kill me. But God saved me from them. Therefore, since God helped me, I've kept on preaching until this day to everyone, rich and poor. Yet I've told them only those things the prophets said would happen: that Jesus would be put to death, and afterwards would rise from the dead, and be a Saviour to the Jews and the Gentiles."

While Paul was speaking, Festus, the governor, said loudly, "Paul, you're crazy. Too much learning has made you mad!"

Paul said, "I'm not mad, most noble Festus. I'm only speaking the truth. King Agrippa understands what I'm saying, for I'm sure he's heard about these things. King Agrippa, do you believe what the prophets wrote? I know you do!"

Then Agrippa said to Paul, "You almost persuade me too, to be a Christian."

Paul said, "I wish that not only you, but all these people who are listening to me this day were Christians like me, except that they wouldn't have to wear these chains!"

When Paul finished speaking, Agrippa stood up, and so did Festus and the chief men of the city who were with them, and they went alone to talk with each other, and said, "This man hasn't done anything for which he should be put to death, or even kept in prison."

Then Agrippa said to Festus, "He could have been set free if he'd not asked to be taken to Rome before Caesar."

When the time came for Paul to be sent to the Emperor Nero in Rome, Festus gave him into the custody of a centurion, who took soldiers with him to guard Paul and some other prisoners on the way there. They went onboard a ship sailing from Caesarea, and reached the city of Sidon the next day. They stopped in Sidon for a while, and the centurion, whose name was Julius, treated Paul well, letting him go ashore to visit some of his friends,

After leaving Sidon they came to the city of Myra. There the centurion took his prisoners onboard another ship in which they set sail for Rome. After sailing slowly for several days they reached a place called the Fair Havens, in the island of Crete. By this time it was winter, and the time for storms.

Paul said to the men on the ship, "Listen, I can see that while we're on this voyage there will be great danger, not only to the ship, but also to our lives."

But the master of the ship, because he didn't believe what Paul said, and didn't think the Fair Havens was a good harbour to stay in for the winter, made up his mind to leave it and try to reach a place called Phenice. When a wind blew gently from the south, the sailors thought they would be able to manage this. So they left the Fair Havens and sailed out to sea.

Soon a strong wind beat against the ship. When the sailors were unable to steer, they let the ship go wherever the wind took it. They came near to an island called Clauda, and there the small boat that was fastened behind the ship was nearly washed away. As soon as they'd managed to take it out of the water, they wound cables, or chains underneath and all around the ship, to keep it from breaking to pieces.

Still being thrown around by the storm, they had to throw some of the cargo into the sea to make the ship lighter, and save it from sinking. The next day they threw over all the ropes and sails that could be spared.

The gale kept blowing, and for several days they couldn't even see the sun in the daytime, or the moon and stars at night, because heavy clouds covered the sky. Most of the crew and passengers thought the ship was going to sink and they'd all be lost.

They had eaten nothing for a long time, and Paul stood up, and said, "Men, you should have listened to me and stayed at the island of Crete, then you wouldn't have been in this great danger. Yet I'm telling you now not to be afraid, for there'll be no loss of life among you; but only of the ship. Last night an angel came to me from God — the God I worship and to whom I belong. The angel spoke to me, and said, 'Don't be afraid, Paul. You will reach Rome safely and be brought before Caesar.' For your sake, God will save the lives of all the men who are with you in the ship. So cheer up, because I believe what the angel told me. Even so, we're going to be shipwrecked on an island."

When the fourteenth night came, as the ship was driven along by the wind, the sailors sensed they were near land. After measuring the depth of water with a line, they found they were right.

Afraid they would hit the rocks on the sea bed, they dropped four anchors to keep the ship from being driven any further, and then waited for the morning. But the sailors, believing the ship would soon be broken to pieces, let down the small boat into the sea, intending to escape in it and leave everyone else to drown.

But Paul said to the centurion, "Unless these sailors stay in the ship, the rest of us cannot be saved."

Then the soldiers cut the ropes that held the small boat, and let it float away without anyone in it.

Before it was light, Paul begged everyone to have something to eat. He said, "This is the fourteenth day since the storm came, and you've hardly eaten anything. Please, eat some food, so you won't get ill. I assure you, no harm will come to any of you."

Then Paul took bread and thanked God for it in front of everyone, and began to eat. Then everyone else ate with him. There were 276 people onboard the ship, and after they'd eaten they threw some more of their cargo of wheat into the sea to lighten the ship even more.

When it was daylight they could see the shore, although they were unable to tell what country this was. Seeing a bay a little way off, they decided to try to steer the ship into it. After they had taken up the anchors and hoisted the sail, they steered towards it, but before they reached it the ship ran aground. The front was stuck on the sea bed, and couldn't be moved. Soon the back of the ship was smashed by the waves that crashed against it.

The soldiers advised the centurion to have the prisoners

killed, because they were afraid some of them would escape. But the centurion, wanting to keep Paul safe, stopped them harming the prisoners, and ordered anyone who could swim to jump into the sea and swim to the shore. The rest, some floating on boards, and some on broken pieces of the ship, followed them. So it was that they all reached land safely.

They discovered they were shipwrecked on an island called Melita (present day Malta). The people of the island welcomed them and lit a fire for them, because of the rain and the cold. Paul gathered a bundle of sticks and put them on the fire, but a poisonous snake came out of the heat and bit onto his hand.

When the people of the island saw the snake hanging on Paul's hand, they said to each other, "This man must be a murderer. He didn't drown in the sea, so now he's being punished by the snake for what he's done."

But Paul shook the snake off into the fire and felt no harm. Then they looked at him for a long time, expecting his arm to swell up, or that he'd fall down dead. When they saw nothing happen, they changed their minds and said he was a god.

The chief of the island, whose name was Publius, invited Paul and those who were with him to his house, where they stayed for three days, being well treated there. The father of Publius was seriously ill with a fever, and Paul laid his hands on him and made him well. When he'd done this, others who were sick in the island came and were also healed. They showed their thanks by giving Paul and his friends presents of things they needed.

After three months, the centurion took Paul and the other prisoners onboard a ship that had been sheltering at the island until the winter was over. In it, and they sailed away to the city of Puteoli in Italy, stopping a couple of times on the way. In Puteoli they stayed seven days with some Christians who lived there. Then they travelled by land to Rome.

When the Christians in Rome heard Paul was on his way, they went out to meet him at a place called the Three Taverns. After Paul had seen them, he gave thanks because he'd been saved from so many dangers, and he knew in his heart that God would still take care of him.

When they reached Rome, the centurion gave the prisoners into the custody of the Roman government, but Paul was allowed to live in a house with a soldier who watched him closely, but the chains he had worn for so long were not taken off.

After three days, Paul sent for the chief men among the Jews who lived in Rome, and said to them, "Men and brothers, I have not done anything wrong to the Jews, nor have I disobeyed the laws which Moses gave to our forefathers. But the Jews at Jerusalem handed me over as a prisoner to the Romans, who, when they questioned me, would have let me go back to Jerusalem because they knew I'd done nothing for which I deserved to die. But the Jews still wanted to kill me, so I asked to be taken before Caesar. I've sent for you to come here so I could see you and talk to you. I'm wearing these chains because I believe in the Saviour, the Messiah about whom the prophets have written."

When he said this, the Jews told him, "We've had no letters sent to us about you, and the Jews who've come here from Jerusalem don't speak anything bad about you. We'd like to hear what it is you preach. As for these Christians, we know they're spoken against everywhere."

After they had agreed a day, many of the Jews came to Paul's house and he taught them, explaining from morning until the evening what the prophets had written about Jesus. Some believed the things he told them, and some didn't believe.

While they differed among themselves, Paul told them that the prophet Isaiah had spoken the truth when he said that although a message from God should be brought to the people of Israel, they wouldn't listen to it because their hearts were wrong, and they didn't want to be His children. So Paul told them that the good news of Jesus which the Jews refused to believe would be preached to the Gentiles, and the Gentiles, he said, would obey it.

Paul stayed two years in Rome, and lived in a house which he hired for himself. There he welcomed everyone who came to hear him, and he taught them about Jesus boldly, for no one tried to stop him.

The Bible does not say where Paul went after this, or how he died. But from accounts given in other books in the New Testament, and from the later writings of the historian Eusebius, it is thought that Paul was set free in Rome and went back to Jerusalem, and then travelled through other countries preaching the good news, until he returned to Rome.

Not many years after this, there was a great fire in Rome, which continued burning for several days. The people believed that their evil emperor, Nero, had ordered the city to be set on fire. To save himself from the blame, Nero accused the Christians of doing it. Then the people rose up in a anger against the Christians, and put many of them to death. Among those who were killed, historians believe, were the apostles Peter and Paul. Paul, tradition says, was beheaded. Peter, it is believed, was crucified upside down because he said he was not worthy to be crucified in the way Jesus was.

Paul would probably have been beheaded and not crucified, because it was against the law to crucify a Roman. But Peter wasn't a free Roman.

It made no difference to these godly men how they died. They knew they would be taken to heaven. And so anyone, who hopes to meet them, will be taken there if they also are followers of Jesus. But if people are not His disciples, then He says to them, as He said to the Jews who refused to believe in Him, "You can't go where I'm going."

The Epistles

AFTER the Acts of the Apostles, come the Epistles. An epistle is a letter, and the Epistles in the New Testament are letters written by the apostles. Some of them were written for particular churches, some were sent to all the churches where there were Christians, and some were written to individual people, but they were passed around and read by many.

When Jesus sent out the apostles to teach the people in all countries, He gave them the Holy Spirit to tell them what to speak and what to write. The unrecorded words the apostles spoke are forgotten, and so are the people who heard them. But people today can still read in the Epistles the words the apostles wrote.

There are twenty-one Epistles. Paul wrote most of them, Peter two, John three, James one, and Jude, or Thaddeus, one. The writer of the Epistle to the Hebrews does not give their name, although early English translations of the Bible say it is Paul. However, over the centuries several other names have been suggested. Perhaps it's not important to know the name of the author. Like the rest of the Bible, the Epistles are a message from God, not from men; and they are intended as much for us as for the people they were sent to at the time. Whatever the Epistles teach, Christians are to believe, to remember, and obey.

The Epistle writers teach that everyone in the world, being born with sinful hearts, has sinned against God. They would all be punished for their sins, if God had not loved them so much that He sent His only Son, Jesus, to be punished in their place. But not everyone is automatically forgiven, but only those who believe and trust in Jesus. How can we tell who believes and trusts in Him? Someone may say they believe when they don't. The Epistles say we can tell by the way someone behaves. If they believe in Jesus, they will love Him, and follow His teaching.

The Epistle writers explain how Christians ought to live, and what sort of people they should be. Christians should be honest, hard working, have self-control, be unassuming; good to the poor; kind to anyone who is unkind to them; not speaking bad things about anyone; loving and forgiving each other; trying to persuade others to be Christians; thankful for their blessings; patient when they have troubles; full of joy, because they are saved; hating what's wrong; loving what's good; praying regularly; and working hard in everything they say and do, to please God.

But Christians can't do these things by themselves, for although they want to do them, Satan is always tempting them to sin. He is their great enemy who, the apostle Peter says, is going about like a roaring lion, seeking to destroy them. But Christians have a Saviour who is stronger. Jesus came on the earth to die for them, and now He watches over them. He hears their prayers, and helps them fight against Satan's ways. And when they fall into sin, if they ask for forgiveness, He asks God to forgive them. And He now lives within His followers as the Holy Spirit, giving them His strength and guidance.

Jesus does more than this. Because people have no righteousness, or goodness of their own to make God pleased with them, He gives them *His* righteousness, and God counts it the same as if it were theirs, exactly as if they'd never sinned. At the last day God will accept all those who have His righteousness, and will take them up to heaven where Jesus is, and where they will never be tempted to sin anymore.

The Epistles warn that as the end of the world draws near, there will be people who make fun of the Bible. They will say, "If Jesus is coming again to judge the world, as the Bible says He is, why is He taking so long?" They won't believe the true reason, which is that God is waiting to give sinful people time to repent, because He's not willing that anyone should be lost, but that everyone can come to Jesus to say sorry for their sins, and have everlasting life.

Although God has waited so long, He won't wait for ever. The Epistle writers warn that the day of the Lord — that is when He comes back and every eye will see Him — will come like a thief comes in the night, when no one is expecting it. The world, with its mighty kingdoms, its splendid cities, and all the great and beautiful things men have made, will be burned up. Then the people who have lived in it will rise up from their graves to be judged.

And now, because God has told this, people who are Christians should be careful to live for Jesus, so when the day of the Lord does come, and Jesus descends to the earth again, they will be ready to meet Him, like the five wise virgins in the parable Jesus told.

We have read in the Gospels and in the book of the Acts that Jesus is God, and that the Holy Spirit is God. We are taught this again in the Epistles. We are taught that God the Father, God the Son, and God the Holy Spirit are three who rule over all things. Yet there are not three Gods, but the three together are one God. We cannot understand this any more than we can understand how God never had a beginning, or how He is in every place at one time; but we can believe it, because the Bible tells us it's so.

It is God the Father who made us; it is God the Son who died for us; it is God the Holy Spirit who comes into our hearts and helps us love and obey the Father and the Son — that is, who makes us Christians. We need not be afraid of worshipping one more than the other, for they are all God. When we pray to Jesus, we pray to God. When we pray to the Holy Spirit, we pray to God. And when we pray to the God the Father, we pray to the Father, the Son, and the Holy Spirit – the Trinity.

The Revelation of Saint John

THE last book in the Bible is called Revelation. It was written by the apostle John when he was very old. One of the evil emperors of Rome, Domitian, was angry because John preached the gospel. So he sent him to a remote island called Patmos. There, tradition says, he was treated cruelly and made to work in the mines, in spite of his great age.

But while John was on Patmos, Jesus came to him in a vision, and showed him the things that John has written down for us in the Book of Revelation. John says, "I heard a loud Voice behind me, like a trumpet. I turned to see who was speaking to me, and I saw Jesus dressed in a robe that reached down to His feet, and on His chest was a golden breastplate."

When John saw Jesus he was afraid, and fell down like someone dead; but Jesus placed His right hand on him, and said, "Don't be afraid. I am First, I am Last. I am the One who was crucified; but, look, I am alive again, and will live for ever".

Jesus talked with John, and gave him messages to seven different churches in Asia, and told him to write down the messages in a book, and send them to the seven churches for which they were intended.

What is one of the best known promises of Jesus is here, in chapter 3, where Jesus is sending a message to the people in the church in Laodicea who are only lukewarm in their faith. He says He's standing at the door of their lives and knocking. If anyone opens the door and lets Him in, He promises to come in and live with that person, as He does to everyone today. In the John chapter 6, He promises He will never turn away anyone who comes to Him.

Then John saw a door in heaven opened wide and a voice called to him, "Come up here, and I will show you what will happen in the future." John heard the voices of a great crowd of angels praising the Saviour, and calling him 'The Lamb that was slain.'

Then, in the vision, John was shown many breathtaking things, to teach him what would happen to Christians on the earth, from that time until the end of the world. He was shown how evil nations and kings would persecute Christians, and kill them, hoping that none of them would be left. But John was also shown how the Lord would destroy those nations and kings, and save His people, so at the end no enemy could hurt them.

After this, John saw a great white throne in heaven, with Jesus sitting on it. He saw the dead rising up from their graves; and they came and stood before the throne to be judged. Then the books were opened in which was written down everything they'd done while they were living on the earth. And the people were judged out of the books from what was written there. Another book was then opened, called the Book of Life. In it were the names of those who had believed and trusted in Jesus. And whoever didn't have their names written in the book of life was cast into the lake of fire.

After the Judgment was over, John saw new skies and a new earth, for the old earth and the skies were burned up. He saw a beautiful city, called the New Jerusalem, coming down out of heaven, and heard a voice say, "God is coming to live with His people."

Around the city was a long, high wall, with twelve gates.

An angel guarded each gate. The city was built of pure gold; in its walls were all kinds of precious stones, and its gates were made of pearls. There was no need for the sun or the moon to light it, for God was there, and the Lord Jesus and the glory that shone around them made it light.

John was shown that the people Jesus has saved from every country will come and live in it. The gates will never be shut, for there will be no night-time there. And none of the sinful will go into it, but only those whose names are written in the Lamb's Book of Life.

John saw also a pure river of water, called the Water of Life. By the side of the river, as it flowed through the streets of the city, grew the Tree of Life bearing twelve different kinds of fruit which ripened every month. Jesus told John that people who live in the city and drink from the River, and eat the fruit from the Tree of Life, will see the Lord's face and be with Him and serve Him.

He will wipe away all the tears from their eyes, and there will be no more death, or pain, or sadness, because all this will have gone for ever.

Jesus says that only those who have washed their robes in the blood of the Lamb will have the right to the Tree of Life, and will enter the city through the gates.

<><><>

One way in which God speaks to us is through His word, the Bible. If you have felt Jesus calling you to follow Him as you've been reading this book, and you don't yet know Him as your Lord and Saviour, you're invited to pray this prayer.

"Lord God, I don't know why You want me to talk to You, but please hear me. There's nothing in my life that could make You love me, but I'm reaching out to You just the same. I turn away from all that's wrong in my life. The

Bible says that Your Son Jesus Christ died on the Cross to take the punishment for all the wrong things in people's lives, and now I want You to make that count for me. Please forgive me for all that's wrong in my life, things now and in the past. Let Jesus be my Saviour, and make me a member of Your family — not just for now, but for eternity."

No matter whether you've been a Christian for a long or a short time, it's important to read the Bible, not just a paraphrase like this. This book is to help explain what's in the New Testament, but it's not a direct translation. The Bible is the true Word of God. Here's the link to the page of helpful Bible reading aids mentioned at the beginning:

Part 2

Running Through the Bible

by

Chris Wright

Part 2 Contents

Running Through the Bible

Author's Note

Due to copyright restrictions, it is not possible to quote from just a single translation of the Bible in *Running Through the Bible* in this section of this book. Selecting two translations has not been easy, because many people have a favourite translation, maybe one that they believe to be the most reliable or easiest to understand.

I have chosen two English translations widely used today: the New International Version NIV), and the English Standard Version ESV). The version used in each quote is marked with its Bible reference at the end of every chapter.

I'm not suggesting that other translations are inferior in any way. Please feel free to look up the references in your own Bible. I support a statement from the introduction of the King James (Authorised) Bible of 1611 — a translation still widely used and loved today — where the translators state: We do not deny, nay we affirm and avow, that the very meanest [poorest] translation of the Bible in English, set forth by men of our profession [professing our faith] ... containeth the word of God, nay, is the word of God.

Here are a few suggestions for going deeper. (There are, of course, many other sources.) Visit www.ewordtoday.com for free online Bible reading plans, in several languages, including *The Bible in One Year* with 365 readings arranged in chronological order starting on any date you choose. Reading plans are on www.biblegateway.com. See also www.youversion.com for hundreds of free Bible versions in many languages online.

www.cwr.org.uk and www.scriptureunion.org.uk are just two publishers of daily Bible-reading notes and other useful study material. You will also benefit from a Bible commentary — expensive, but probably a lot cheaper than your phone, tablet or sports kit! If you need help in choosing the most appropriate reading material for yourself, ask your church leader or a Christian bookshop for advice

Chris Wright

Chapter 1

Let me start with a word of warning. If you're in church, and someone at the front asks for hands up from anyone who's read the whole book of Hezekiah, don't be tempted to put your hand up. It's an old trick. There is no book of Hezekiah!

Yes, Hezekiah appears in the Bible. He's a significant person, and we can read one of his prayers, but he didn't write a whole book. Is he:

A great-grandson of Adam and Eve?

A disbelieving uncle of Noah, when God decided to start again with people in the Flood?

A wise servant of Abraham and Sarah, the couple chosen by God to become the ancestors of the people later called the Children of Israel?

One of Jacob's grandsons when the Children of Israel were slaves in Egypt?

A priest who made a golden calf in the desert of Sinai, in defiance of Moses when they escaped from Egypt in the Exodus?

A scheming servant of Samuel, in the time of the Judges that came after Moses?

A priest who blessed King David before a major victory over the Philistines?

A writer of several Psalms?

A prophet who warned King Solomon that his kingdom would be divided in two: Israel with the city of Samaria in the north, and Judah with the city of Jerusalem in the south?

A godly but eventually unwise king who was stupid enough to proudly show the treasures of his palace in Jerusalem to the visiting Babylonians, and not worry about the consequences?

A prophet who later promised the Jews in exile, captured by the Babylonians, that they would one day return to Jerusalem?

A skilled stone mason who helped Nehemiah rebuild Jerusalem and the Temple, seventy years after the Babylonians had destroyed it for the treasures?

A priest in the Temple in Jerusalem who announced the birth of Jesus, the promised Messiah?

A prominent Pharisee who argued with Jesus about Jesus' power and authority to forgive sins?

One of the first men to see Jesus after he rose from the dead after the crucifixion?

A leader of the early Christian church in Antioch?

A scribe who helped the apostle Paul, who was in prison, copy some of his letters to the new churches?

The leader of a failing church condemned by Jesus in the book of Revelation?

We'll find Hezekiah later, but you may be surprised to know that in these few questions we've raced through the Bible from beginning to end, with major events in their correct order, even though Hezekiah was only there for one of them.

If you skimmed through the list because you already know the answer, read it again, carefully this time. You may find you learn a lot from it.

I can't promise that there will be answers in these pages that will help you shine in the obligatory Bible question(s) at your local quiz night, but if you're new to the Bible, I want to give you a clearer idea of the events between its pages.

Chapter 2

The Bible is a massive book and it should be read slowly and carefully — and of course prayerfully. So why are we running through it? Why the rush?

The Bible isn't like a long novel that you pick up to take on holiday, where you start at the beginning and work your way through to the end in just a few days. It's a collection of writings, individual books that took many centuries to put together. The first book, Genesis, records events at the beginning of time and quickly moves on to people who lived several thousand years ago. The last book, Revelation, was written near the end of the first century AD.

All I want to do now is give a flavour of what's between the start of Genesis in the Old Testament, and the end of Revelation in the New Testament. This should help you get to grips with reading the Bible with more understanding.

As you will probably, but not necessarily, know, the Old Testament is the story of God's people before the birth of Jesus. The New Testament tells the birth, life, death and resurrection of Jesus, the Son of God, with writing by leaders of the early Christian church.

If you want to start reading at Genesis chapter 1, that's fine. But if you keep going, you'll soon come to chapter after chapter of names and regulations. Most people new to the Bible quickly lose interest at this point, wrongly assuming that this is the shape of things to come. If they understood the Bible better, they would know which parts are more interesting.

I'm saying more interesting, not more important. Christians believe that the whole Bible is the word of God, so every bit of it is important. But much of it is not for newcomers or the fainthearted to dip into.

So to give this flavour and basic understanding of the Bible, I'm taking verses from various books of the Bible and sometimes abridging them considerably. All direct quotations from the Bible will be in italics. The missing wording will be indicated by ellipses. The full Bible reference is shown immediately after each quotation. The references are often for longer readings than the quoted words. I recommend you read every reference in full later, as a way of getting a better insight of the Bible. Let's start at the very beginning, at Genesis chapter 1.

In the beginning God created the heavens and the earth... . And God said, "Let there be light," and there was light (Genesis 1:1-26 NIV).

Later, we read: *Then God said, "Let us make man in our image, in our likeness, and let them rule over the fish of the sea and the birds of the air, over the livestock, over all the earth, and over all the creatures that move along the ground."* (Genesis 1:26 NIV).

Then at the end of chapter 1: *God saw all that he had made, and it was very good* (Genesis 1:31 NIV)

When God created Adam and Eve — the first people with souls and the ability to know and love God — everything was very good. If God thought it was all very good, then it was. God also gave people free will, allowing them to live a perfect life with him — or go their own way. Probably everyone knows, or can guess, what happens next.

In Genesis 3 it all starts to go wrong. Satan, the enemy of God who was once an angel of light, chose to disobey God and set up his own powerbase with other rebellious angels.

Here, he appears as a snake:

Now the serpent was more crafty than any of the wild animals the Lord God had made. He said to the woman, "Did God really say, 'You must not eat from any tree in the garden'?"

The woman said to the serpent, "We may eat fruit from the trees in the garden, but God did say, 'You must not eat fruit from the tree that is in the middle of the garden, and you must not touch it, or you will die.'"

"You will not surely die," the serpent said to the woman. "For God knows that when you eat of it your eyes will be opened, and you will be like God, knowing good and evil" (Genesis 3:1-5 NIV).

Having their own way seemed like a good idea at the time, but after disobeying God, Adam and Eve feel ashamed and afraid. When God confronts them, they start the blame game.

The man said, "The woman you put here with me — she gave me some fruit from the tree, and I ate it."

Then the Lord God said to the woman, "What is this you have done?"

The woman said, "The serpent deceived me, and I ate."

So the Lord God said to the serpent, "Because you have done this, cursed are you above all the livestock and all the wild animals! You will crawl on your belly and you will eat dust all the days of your life. And I will put enmity between you and the woman, and between your offspring and hers; he will crush your head, and you will strike his heel."

To the woman he said, "I will greatly increase your pains in childbearing; with pain you will give birth to children. Your desire will be for your husband, and he will rule over you."

To Adam he said, "Because you listened to your wife and

ate from the tree about which I commanded you, 'You must not eat of it,' Cursed is the ground because of you; through painful toil you will eat of it all the days of your life.

"It will produce thorns and thistles for you, and you will eat the plants of the field. By the sweat of your brow you will eat your food until you return to the ground, since from it you were taken; for dust you are and to dust you will return" (Genesis 3:12-19 NIV).

I've quoted these verses at length, because it's important to see that although at the start everything was very good, it is people who quickly went wrong. And it's our selfish way of living that is causing so much pain and suffering today. This is not how God planned it, but he allowed it rather than create us as divinely-controlled robots. He wanted them to love him voluntarily, and according to the Bible he still does.

God shows his love for us in that while we were still sinners, Christ died for us (Romans 5:8 NIV).

This is just one of many, many verses in both the Old and New Testaments about God's love for us, and it is the red cord that will run through the Bible from start to finish. Red — the colour of blood. God says that Satan, the devil, will be crushed by the "seed" of a woman — we now know that woman to be the Virgin Mary. Her son Jesus is the seed, the offspring. If you're not at all familiar with the Bible, this comes at the start of the New Testament with the birth of Jesus Christ, the Son of God. Christians believe that Jesus overcame death at his crucifixion. When Jesus rose from the dead, Satan was defeated. But we're getting ahead of ourselves here. Let's see what happens next.

Suggestions on How to Read the Bible

When you read about an event in the Bible, try to imagine you're actually there. What's happening? What is everyone thinking? How are they dressed? How old are the main characters? Is it sunny or raining? Hot or cold? Night or day? This will help you get a better idea of what is going on – even if you imagine some details incorrectly. You need to be there, watching and listening. And be sure to watch out for that red cord.

As soon as you feel ready to go deeper, ask the Holy Spirit to reveal more of God in the pages. Although God can speak to us through individual verses (sometimes verses taken completely out of context), it is better to read whole passages, and see what God is telling us through them, rather than regularly taking a "lucky dip". True understanding of God and his plans for us come from the whole Bible, although we will surely need the help of good Bible teaching.

Bible reading notes, with a passage and thought for each day, are a great way to read the Bible. Ask your church or a Christian bookshop for help in finding the best notes for your age and understanding of the Bible. In other words, some Bible reading notes are simpler or more detailed than others. The choice is yours. See my Author's Note.

Chapter 3

Adam and Eve are not only thrown out of the Garden of Eden, where there has been complete safety and a daily walk with God, they have to put up with problems with their two sons, Cain and Abel. After an argument about which of them brought the better sacrifice to God, Cain ends up killing Abel.

From then on, for several generations, it's mostly downhill for these early people who are not living in the way in which God created them. Eventually God decides that enough is enough. He will start again with a godly man called Noah, along with his family. Yes, it's the story of Noah and the ark.

The Lord saw how great man's wickedness on the earth had become, and that every inclination of the thoughts of his heart was only evil all the time. The Lord was grieved that he had made man on the earth, and his heart was filled with pain... . But Noah found favour in the eyes of the Lord... . Noah was a righteous man, blameless among the people of his time, and he walked with God... . God said to Noah, "I am going to put an end to all people, for the earth is filled with violence because of them. I am surely going to destroy both them and the earth. So make yourself an ark of cypress wood; make rooms in it and coat it with pitch inside and out... . I will establish my covenant with you, and you will enter the ark — you and your sons and your wife and your sons' wives with you... . Noah did everything just as God commanded him (Genesis 5:1-32 NIV).

The flood comes and Noah and his family are safe. Many months later the ark comes to rest and the sun shines. God points to the rainbow and says it stands for a promise that he will never do the same again.

Although Noah wouldn't have known it at the time, the red cord is running through this event, for just as there was safety in the ark, so there is safety in the promised Messiah (Jesus Christ) who will come to earth several thousand years later, the descendant of Eve.

Then: The nations spread out over the earth after the flood. God had instructed Noah to do this with his family and their descendants, but unfortunately they didn't get far. In Babel they stopped and built a tall tower to prove that they were important and could reach heaven — which of course they couldn't manage to do. So the Lord scattered them ... over all the earth. Genesis 10:32 to 11:9 NIV).

When did the events in the Bible happen? In the middle of the seventeenth century, Archbishop James Ussher decided to put some dates into Bible events, and these appear at the top of pages of some older Bibles, both Catholic and Protestant translations. However, they are definitely not part of the original writing, and many of them are now considered wrong.

Archaeologists, geologists and Bible scholars today are coming up with dates that are more reliable than those from earlier researchers. But with some events, such as when Moses was in Egypt, they are still at odds with each other by many years — centuries even. So, interesting though it would be to know exactly when various people lived in the early chapters of the Old Testament, it's not essential that we know, and certainly not worth any bitter disputes. Nowhere in the Bible does it say that a correct understanding of chronology is essential to salvation!

Most Bible scholars are generally in close agreement with the dates from King David onwards (c1000 BC), because the names of many people and places coincide with non-biblical records from surrounding countries.

Most people are familiar with the stages of civilization called the Neolithic, Bronze and Iron Ages. Many used to think that these people were extremely primitive, but modern archaeologists have shown us just how advanced many of them were, by studying recent finds of their pottery, art and ornaments. These ages were also taking place in what we now call the Middle East, but generally happening earlier than the dates of these ages in Europe. Even though one age tended to blur into another, the arrival of advanced technology can be traced from area to area, giving rise to the occasional major advance in civilization.

Early examples of Bronze Age people in the Middle East are Abraham and Sarah. Bible scholars usually date them to around 2000 BC. In a large museum you are likely to find items from the Bronze Age from your local region. In national museums such as the British Museum in London, there are whole displays of amazing goods from what is now Israel and the surrounding countries. These people were certainly not as primitive as once thought.

I find it interesting to speculate what must have been happening in the Bible lands when Stonehenge was built in England, when a local Bronze Age burial mound was first used, and when Iron Age fortifications seen on holiday were built.

If you want to investigate perceived dates of early Bible events for yourself, be prepared to encounter people with very strongly held opinions that are not open to negotiation. I take the view that knowing dates is interesting to me as a Bible reader, but things happened when they happened, and no amount of arguing will make them happen at any other time. The Bible sets out to tell the story of God and his plan for us. It is not a dated calendar or science handbook, and we should not try to make it one.

Chapter 4

At the top of the previous page, I mentioned Abraham and Sarah. They are the founders of the Jewish people. A great nation is promised for the future. The red cord runs through here.

The Lord had said to Abram, "Leave your country, your people and your father's household and go to the land I will show you. I will make you into a great nation and I will bless you; I will make your name great, and you will be a blessing. I will bless those who bless you, and whoever curses you I will curse; and all peoples on earth will be blessed through you." So Abram left, as the Lord had told him; and Lot went with him (Genesis 12 to 14 NIV).

Lot is Abram's nephew. Abram? Yes, it is later that God changes Abram's name to Abraham. Abraham means Father of a Multitude — the father of the promised great nation.

But things don't seem to be working out. Abraham and Sarah are getting older and older, and still no child. Eventually, after an encounter with Three Visitors: The Lord was gracious to Sarah as he had said, and the Lord did for Sarah what he had promised. Sarah became pregnant and bore a son to Abraham in his old age, at the very time God had promised him. Abraham gave the name Isaac to the son Sarah bore him (Genesis 21:1-3 NIV).

We really have to hurry on now, but you can read much more about Abraham in the Bible — including God's test of Abraham's faith by asking him to sacrifice his son, in a country where child sacrifice to foreign gods was not unusual. - Genesis 22:1-19.

Isaac marries Rebekah (Genesis 24:1-67) and they have twin sons Jacob and Esau. Esau is born first:

Isaac was sixty years old when Rebekah gave birth to them. The boys grew up, and Esau became a skilful hunter, a man of the open country, while Jacob was a quiet man, staying among the tents... . Once when Jacob was cooking some stew, Esau came in from the open country, famished. He said to Jacob, "Quick, let me have some of that red stew! I'm famished!" Jacob replied, "First sell me your birthright."

"Look, I am about to die," Esau said. "What good is the birthright to me?"

But Jacob said, "Swear to me first."

So he swore an oath to him, selling his birthright to Jacob. Then Jacob gave Esau some bread and some lentil stew. He ate and drank, and then got up and left. So Esau despised his birthright¬ (Genesis 25:19-34 NIV).

There is now a time of famine, and Isaac and Rebekah are looking to move on.

The Lord appeared to Isaac and said, "Do not go down to Egypt; live in the land where I tell you to live. Stay in this land for a while, and I will be with you and will bless you. For to you and your descendants I will give all these lands and will confirm the oath I swore to your father Abraham. I will make your descendants as numerous as the stars in the sky and will give them all these lands, and through your offspring all nations on earth will be blessed, because Abraham obeyed me and kept my requirements, my commands, my decrees and my laws"(Genesis 26:1-5 NIV).

Jacob, now also called Israel, wrestles with God one night, then goes to make peace with his brother Esau (Genesis 32:22 to 33:30) Jacob has twelve sons (the children of Israel, aka Jacob), but his favourite is Joseph.

Joseph's jealous brothers sell him as a slave and he ends up in Egypt.

After some major setbacks, Joseph comes to the aid of the pharaoh by explaining a dream that no one else can interpret - Genesis 39:1 to 41:57 NIV).

Pharaoh said to Joseph, "I hereby put you in charge of the whole land of Egypt." Then Pharaoh took his signet ring from his finger and put it on Joseph's finger. He dressed him in robes of fine linen and put a gold chain around his neck. He had him ride in a chariot as his second-in-command, and men shouted before him, "Make way!" Thus he put him in charge of the whole land of Egypt (Genesis 37:1-36 NIV).

There is a famine in Egypt and Joseph's brothers come asking for food, not knowing that their brother is not only alive, but is now in charge. Joseph forgives them, and Jacob and his family move to Egypt permanently.

Then Jacob left Beersheba, and Israel's sons took their father Jacob and their children and their wives in the carts that Pharaoh had sent to transport him. They also took with them their livestock and the possessions they had acquired in Canaan, and Jacob and all his offspring went to Egypt. He took with him to Egypt his sons and grandsons and his daughters and granddaughters — all his offspring (Genesis 42:1 to 47:31 NIV).

Chapter 5

As the years pass, the descendants of Jacob (known as Hebrews) become so many, that a later pharaoh decides to kill every Hebrew boy as soon as he are born. But pharaoh's daughter rescues a baby called Moses from the Nile, and brings him up in the royal palace.

Now a man of the house of Levi married a Levite woman, and she became pregnant and gave birth to a son... . When she could hide him no longer, she got a papyrus basket for him and coated it with tar and pitch. Then she placed the child in it and put it among the reeds along the bank of the Nile... . Pharaoh's daughter went down to the Nile to bathe, and ... she saw the basket among the reeds and sent her slave girl to get it... . "This is one of the Hebrew babies," she said... . She called him Moses, saying, "I drew him out of the water" (Exodus 2:11-15 NIV).

When he is a young man, Moses sees the Hebrews who are living in slavery now, and kills an Egyptian who is attacking a Hebrew. But Moses is being watched, and he has to flee to the land of Midian. Lack of space here prevents us looking in detail at what happens next, but God tells Moses to go back to Egypt and bring his people out of slavery, which he does. (Exodus 3:1 to 6:12.)

Now comes a major part of the red cord — God's rescue plan is still running with us. It comes four hundred years after Joseph was taken to Egypt as a slave, after being sold by his brothers, the sons of Jacob. God says that every Hebrew family — also called the Children of Israel (of

Jacob), or Israelites — must kill a lamb or goat and wipe the blood over their door posts, to protect them from his anger in the coming night when God passes over. This will then be called the Passover, for obvious reasons, and will later become a picture for Christians of the blood of Jesus on the Cross sheltering them from God's judgment.

Each man is to take a lamb for his family, one for each household... . Then they are to take some of the blood and put it on the sides and tops of the doorframes of the houses where they eat the lambs... . Eat it in haste; it is the Lord's Passover. On that same night I will pass through Egypt and strike down every firstborn — both men and animals — and I will bring judgment on all the gods of Egypt. I am the Lord. The blood will be a sign for you on the houses where you are; and when I see the blood, I will pass over you. No destructive plague will touch you when I strike Egypt" (Exodus 12:1-13 NIV).

Having fled from Egypt, the Israelites are wandering in a desert, short of food. It's not long before they begin to complain, and remember the "good times" in slavery.

In the desert the whole community grumbled against Moses and Aaron. The Israelites said to them, "If only we had died by the Lord's hand in Egypt! There we sat around pots of meat and ate all the food we wanted, but you have brought us out into this desert to starve this entire assembly to death." Then the Lord said to Moses, "I will rain down bread from heaven for you." ... So Moses and Aaron said to all the Israelites, "In the evening you will know that it was the Lord who brought you out of Egypt, and in the morning you will see the glory of the Lord, because he has heard your grumbling against him... . You are not grumbling against us, but against the Lord"(Exodus 16 NIV).

Which is exactly what happens. In the desert, God gives

Moses the Ten Commandments (Exodus 20:1-17), with many rules and regulations for living in such hot and crowded conditions. The Israelites are close to the border of the land promised to Abraham — the Promised Land — but they are afraid to occupy it. Instead of trusting God, they make idols and worship them.

God instructs Moses to make a small ark (a box carried on poles) to contain the stones on which the Ten Commandments are written, and he also gives instructions on making a portable tent for sacrifice and worship. (Exodus 36:1 to 40:38.)

Racing on forty years, Moses is dead and his right-hand man Joshua takes charge.

After the death of Moses the servant of the Lord, the Lord said to Joshua son of Nun, Moses' aide: "Moses my servant is dead. Now then, you and all these people, get ready to cross the Jordan River into the land I am about to give to them — to the Israelites. I will give you every place where you set your foot, as I promised Moses" (Joshua 1:1-3 NIV).

Joshua prepares to occupy the land, but needs to know what lies ahead.

Then Joshua son of Nun secretly sent two spies... . They went and entered the house of a prostitute called Rahab and stayed there. The king of Jericho was told, "Look! Some of the Israelites have come here tonight to spy out the land."

So the king of Jericho sent this message to Rahab: "Bring out the men who came to you and entered your house, because they have come to spy out the whole land."

But the woman had taken the two men and hidden them... . Before the spies lay down for the night, she went up on the roof and said to them, "I know that the Lord has given this land to you and that a great fear of you has fallen on us, so that all who live in this country are melting in fear because of you... . For the Lord your God is God in heaven above and on the earth below. Now then, please swear to me by the Lord that you will show kindness to my family, because I have shown kindness to you. Give me a sure sign that you will spare the lives of my father and mother, my brothers and sisters, and all who belong to them, and that you will save us from death" (Joshua 2:1-24 NIV).

Rahab is told to hang a red cord from her window when the Israelites come. The attacking Israelite soldiers will see the cord and keep the family safe. Our own red cord runs clearly through this episode, echoing the protection from the blood on the doorposts at the Exodus from Egypt with Moses, and foretelling the protection through death of Jesus in the New Testament.

Then the two men started back. They went down out of the hills, forded the river and came to Joshua son of Nun and told him everything that had happened to them.

They said to Joshua, "The Lord has surely given the whole land into our hands; all the people are melting in fear because of us."

Rahab the prostitute will become an ancestor of the great King David, and an ancestor of Mary the mother of Jesus. So Rahab, famous for her own red cord, has a major role in God's plans, and is an example of how God sometimes uses what seem to be the most unlikely and undeserving people.

Jericho falls (literally) and Rahab is kept safe. Having seen that they're on the winning side with God, you would think that the Israelites would be full of praise and worship. Instead, they start to follow the gods of the people they have conquered. After many setbacks, the Promised Land is finally divided among the twelve tribes, the descendants of

Jacob, the Children of Israel.

Now these are the areas the Israelites received as an inheritance in the land of Canaan, which Eleazar the priest, Joshua son of Nun and the heads of the tribal clans of Israel allotted to them (Joshua 14:1 to 21:45 NIV).

Age catches up with Joshua, and he says farewell to the people he has led from the desert into the land that God promised to Abraham several hundred years earlier.

"Be very strong; be careful to obey all that is written in the Book of the Law of Moses, without turning aside to the right or to the left. Do not associate with these nations that remain among you; do not invoke the names of their gods or swear by them. You must not serve them or bow down to them. But you are to hold fast to the Lord your God, as you have until now. The Lord has driven out before you great and powerful nations; to this day no one has been able to withstand you. One of you routs a thousand, because the Lord your God fights for you, just as he promised. So be very careful to love the Lord your God" (Joshua 23:1 to 24:33 NIV).

If you've been observing how God's people often go wrong, you'll know what Joshua probably suspects will happen once they enter the Promised Land: the people will find the foreign gods, with their associated sex worship, to be extremely attractive.

Then the Israelites did evil in the eyes of the Lord and served the Baals. They forsook the Lord, the God of their fathers, who had brought them out of Egypt. They followed and worshipped various gods of the peoples around them. They provoked the Lord to anger because they forsook him and served Baal and the Ashtoreths. In his anger against Israel the Lord handed them over to raiders who plundered them. He sold them to their enemies all around, whom they were no longer able to resist. Whenever Israel went out to fight, the hand of the Lord was against them to defeat them, just as he had sworn to them. They were in great distress (Judges 2:11-15 NIV).

Chapter 6

God calls a young man called Gideon to help his people. (Judges 6:1 to 7:25.) After Gideon's death, various judges are called on, and one of the most famous judges is Samson. (Judges 13:1 to 16:31.) More fighting and infighting follows Samson's dramatic death.

Later: In the days when the judges ruled there was a famine in the land, and a man of Bethlehem in Judah went to sojourn in the country of Moab, he and his wife and his two sons. (Read the whole book of Ruth - ESV quoted here).

We are about to run across the red cord again, because Naomi, the wife, is left a widow in the land of Moab, with both her sons also dead. One of her sons has married a local girl called Ruth. Ruth, although from Moab, and brought up to worship Moabite gods with the cult of child sacrifice, returns to Bethlehem with Naomi when the famine is over, and falls in love with one of Naomi's relatives, called Boaz.

So Boaz took Ruth, and she became his wife. And he went in to her, and the Lord gave her conception, and she bore a son. Then the women said to Naomi, "Blessed be the Lord, who has not left you this day without a redeemer, and may his name be renowned in Israel!"

Their descendants certainly did become famous. Ruth and Boaz are ancestors of King David, and of Mary the mother of Jesus. Rahab, a prostitute. Ruth, a woman from a country worshipping evil gods. Keep following the red cord.

Many years later, a woman called Hannah is praying for a child, and promises God that if she conceives, she will give the child to God.

She said to her husband, "As soon as the child is weaned, I will bring him, so that he may appear in the presence of the Lord and dwell there forever." (Read 1 Samuel 1:1 to 2:11).

The details are something you will have to read for yourself in 1 and 2 Samuel. Samuel is persuaded to give the people a king, much against his advice. Saul is chosen and anointed. But Saul does not turn out to be a good choice, and David, a shepherd boy subsequently anointed by Samuel, is standing by to take Saul's place. David kills the Philistine giant Goliath, and this makes Saul jealous rather than grateful. (Read 1 Samuel 17:1 to 19:24).

After the death of Saul, and under the rule of David, the twelve tribes live in relative harmony in their own territory, coming together to fight other nations as and when necessary.

Another distant ancestor of Mary comes onto the stage — Bathsheba. After committing adultery with Bathsheba, King David arranges to have her husband, Uriah, killed in battle. David and Bathsheba are both ancestors of Mary. With skeletons like Rahab, Ruth from Moab, and Bathsheba in the cupboard, it would have been easy for the writers of the Old Testament to leave out the embarrassing parts. The fact that names like these are included in the history of the Israelites, and also mentioned in the New Testament, is a clear indication of the reliability of what we read.

David, such an important person in God's plans, in spite of his many failures, is described by the apostle Paul as a man after God's own heart. (See Acts 13:22). David wrote many of the Psalms in the Old Testament, but certainly not all of them. Some go back as far as the time of Moses. David's Psalms often centre on repentance.

David wants to capture Jerusalem, to make it God's city.

The king and his men went to Jerusalem against the Jebusites, the inhabitants of the land, who said to David, "You will not come in here, but the blind and the lame will ward you off" — thinking, "David cannot come in here." Nevertheless, David took the stronghold of Zion, that is, the city of David (2 Samuel 5:6-7 ESV).

David would like to build a permanent Temple in Jerusalem, but because of his past life and the bloodshed in battle after battle, the prophet Nathan has to give David this message from God:

I will give you rest from all your enemies. Moreover, the Lord declares to you that the Lord will make you a house. When your days are fulfilled and you lie down with your fathers, I will raise up your offspring after you, who shall come from your body, and I will establish his kingdom. He shall build a house for my name, and I will establish the throne of his kingdom forever (2 Samuel 7:11-13 ESV).

The offspring referred to here is Solomon, one of David's sons from Bathsheba. Solomon was known as a wise king, and he gathered many proverbs in the book of that name.

When David's time to die drew near, he commanded Solomon his son, saying, "... Keep the charge of the Lord your God, walking in his ways and keeping his statutes, his commandments, his rules, and his testimonies, ... that the Lord may establish his word that he spoke concerning me, saying, 'If your sons pay close attention to their way, to walk before me in faithfulness with all their heart and with all their soul, you shall not lack a man on the throne of Israel'" (1 Kings 2:1-4 ESV).

Solomon, portrayed as the wisest king ever (2 Chronicles 1:1-13), built the Temple in Jerusalem, saw the Queen of Sheba, and made many wise decisions. But eventually ...

Now King Solomon loved many foreign women ... from the nations concerning which the Lord had said to the people of Israel, "You shall not enter into marriage with them, neither shall they with you, for surely they will turn away your heart after their gods." ... When Solomon was old his wives turned away his heart after other gods, and his heart was not wholly true to the Lord his God, as was the heart of David his father... . Therefore the Lord said to Solomon, "Since this has been your practice and you have not kept my covenant and my statutes that I have commanded you, I will surely tear the kingdom from you... . Yet for the sake of David your father I will not do it in your days, but I will tear it out of the hand of your son" (1 Kings 11:1-12 ESV).

Following the death of Solomon, the kingdom of the twelve tribes splits into two factions: ten tribes of Israel in the north with Samaria as their capital city; and two tribes of Judah and Benjamin in the south, with Jerusalem as their capital. Each country has a succession of their own kings, both good and bad.

In Israel, in the time of King Ahab, two mighty prophets, Elijah (1 Kings 16:29 to 2 Kings 1:18) and Elisha (2 Kings 2:1 to 13:25), perform great signs of God's power, but with little lasting effect. After the death of Elisha, God seems to give up on Israel, allowing the Assyrians to invade and finally capture the whole country, taking the people into captivity.

The red cord appears to be broken in the north, while in the southern kingdom of Judah the people mistakenly believe that God will protect them, no matter what they get up to. This is where the southern prophets play a major role.

Jeremiah is a major prophet in Judah, up to the fall of Jerusalem and the captivity by the Babylonians. He has a whole book of his prophecies and warnings in the Bible.

Jeremiah tells the people that they are like an unfaithful wife, or children completely out of control, so judgment is inevitable — and the only thanks he gets for passing on God's message is imprisonment! However, he does have good news for the future, but for after 70 years in exile.

We can read about the troubles in Israel and Judah, with their kings and prophets, in the books of Kings and Chronicles.

Chapter 7

When I started reading the Bible on my own, it took me a long time to understand how the accounts of the kings and prophets fitted together. The history of the kings is told in the books of Kings and Chronicles. The books of the prophets are listed together in our Bibles, and arranged in order of length or perceived importance, rather than date. Hence my (and maybe your) confusion. The books of the prophets cover the 300 or so years following the reign of Solomon, when there were the two kingdoms — large Israel in the north and smaller Judah with Benjamin in the south.

The prophet Amos spoke to both kingdoms around 767 to 753 BC, before Assyria invaded. Isaiah and Micah followed him in Judah, while Hosea was working in the northern kingdom. Their messages were that the people and their towns and cities would be destroyed unless they repented and turned back to God. How right they were.

Hosea is the last recorded prophet in Israel. The Assyrians, who have already captured much of Israel, sweep down on Samaria almost as soon as Hosea has finished preaching, destroying the city and taking the people captive. We don't hear much more about them. By the time of Jesus, the inhabitants are called Samaritans, despised by the Jews as being descended from Jewish and Assyrian stock, worshipping with a mixture of Jewish and pagan beliefs.

Modern Israel includes much of the land that became Judah and Israel after the reign of Solomon, which may cause some confusion when reading the Old Testament unless you are aware of this.

In the south, Isaiah and Micah were busy warning the people of Judah that they would suffer the same fate as neighbouring Israel if they didn't turn back to God. Over the next hundred or more years, sometimes they repented, sometimes they didn't. Some kings of Judah encouraged the worship of God, others were more interested in pagan gods. Their danger was to come not from the Assyrians, but from the emerging power of Babylon.

The prophets Nahum, Joel, Habakkuk and Zephaniah give clear warnings to the two tribes in Judah, which are ignored, and the final destruction of Jerusalem comes in 586 BC, at the end of the prophet Jeremiah's time. All except the poorest people are taken to Babylon. The prophet Ezekiel covers both the fall and the captivity. Daniel is one of the captives in what is known as the Exile.

The last king of Israel is Hoshea (c732-722 BC), and the last king of Judah is Zedekiah (c597-586 BC). Both kings are ruling when their countries fall to the invaders, but many years apart.

Hezekiah (729-686 BC) — you may remember him from the quiz in chapter one — is the fifth king of Judah after Solomon, during the time of the prophets Isaiah and Micah. You can read about the kings and prophets in the books of Kings and Chronicles, and of course about the prophets in the Old Testament books of their names.

Only one possible answer in the quiz about Hezekiah in chapter one is correct. He was indeed a wise king, one who did much to bring the people back to God, but ultimately foolish and selfish.

Hezekiah has to deal with the Assyrians, and pay them to leave his country alone. He consults the prophet Isaiah at this point. Here is a heavily abridged account of one of

Isaiah's meetings with King Hezekiah. I urge you to read the whole reference, and not just this abridged portion. I have taken up the rest of the chapter with an account of Judah at this time, as it will help with understanding Bible history by discovering how real it is. Don't forget to imagine you're there, watching and listening. So what do you see and hear?

In the fourteenth year of King Hezekiah, Sennacherib king of Assyria came up against all the fortified cities of Judah and took them. And Hezekiah king of Judah sent to the king of Assyria at Lachish, saying, "I have done wrong; withdraw from me. Whatever you impose on me I will bear."

And the king of Assyria required of Hezekiah king of Judah three hundred talents of silver and thirty talents of gold. And Hezekiah gave him all the silver that was found in the house of the Lord and in the treasuries of the king's house (ESV). Read 2 Kings 18:13 to 19:36 for the whole reading.

It seems that the payment is not enough to keep the Assyrians away. This message is shouted out in Hebrew below the walls of Jerusalem, so that everyone, not just Hezekiah, can hear and understand.

"Hear the word of the great king, the king of Assyria! Thus says the king: 'Do not let Hezekiah deceive you, for he will not be able to deliver you out of my hand. Do not let Hezekiah make you trust in the Lord by saying, 'The Lord will surely deliver us, and this city will not be given into the hand of the king of Assyria.' ... Has any of the gods of the nations ever delivered his land out of the hand of the king of Assyria?" ...

Hezekiah also gets the threat of invasion in writing:

Hezekiah received the letter from the hand of the messengers and read it; and Hezekiah went up to the house of the Lord and spread it before the Lord. And Hezekiah prayed before the Lord and said: "O Lord, the God of Israel, enthroned above the cherubim, you are the God, you alone, of all the kingdoms of the earth; you have made heaven and earth. Incline your ear, O Lord, and hear; open your eyes, O Lord, and see; and hear the words of Sennacherib, which he has sent to mock the living God. Truly, O Lord, the kings of Assyria have laid waste the nations and their lands and have cast their gods into the fire, for they were not gods, but the work of men's hands, wood and stone. Therefore they were destroyed. So now, O Lord our God, save us, please, from his hand, that all the kingdoms of the earth may know that you, O Lord, are God alone." ...

Then Isaiah the son of Amoz sent to Hezekiah, saying, "Thus says the Lord, the God of Israel: Your prayer to me about Sennacherib king of Assyria I have heard.... . Therefore thus says the Lord concerning the king of Assyria: He shall not come into this city or shoot an arrow there, or come before it with a shield or cast up a siege mound against it. By the way that he came, by the same he shall return, and he shall not come into this city, declares the Lord. For I will defend this city to save it, for my own sake and for the sake of my servant David."

And that night the angel of the Lord went out and struck down 185,000 in the camp of the Assyrians. And when people arose early in the morning, behold, these were all dead bodies. Then Sennacherib king of Assyria departed and went home and lived at Nineveh.

When he returns home, Sennacherib is assassinated by his sons. Later on, Hezekiah's pride is to lead to Jerusalem's eventual downfall. Although the Temple and royal palace have been stripped of much of their silver and gold to pay off the Assyrians, Hezekiah boasts about the remaining treasures in his palace, to a group of Babylonian officials on a state visit. How their eyes must have lit up.

At that time Merodach-baladan the son of Baladan, king of Babylon, sent envoys with letters and a present to Hezekiah, for he heard that Hezekiah had been sick. And Hezekiah welcomed them, and he showed them all his treasure house, the silver, the gold, the spices, the precious oil, his armoury, all that was found in his storehouses. There was nothing in his house or in all his realm that Hezekiah did not show them.

Then Isaiah the prophet came to King Hezekiah, and said to him, "What did these men say? And from where did they come to you?"

And Hezekiah said, "They have come from a far country, from Babylon."

He said, "What have they seen in your house?"

And Hezekiah answered, "They have seen all that is in my house; there is nothing in my storehouses that I did not show them."

Then Isaiah said to Hezekiah, "Hear the word of the Lord: Behold, the days are coming, when all that is in your house, and that which your fathers have stored up until this day, shall be carried to Babylon. Nothing shall be left, says the Lord. And some of your own sons, who shall be born to you, shall be taken away, and they shall be eunuchs in the palace of the king of Babylon."

Then said Hezekiah to Isaiah, "The word of the Lord that you have spoken is good." For he thought, "Why not, if there will be peace and security in my days?" (2 Kings 20:12–19 ESV).

Hezekiah's desire to worship God did not rub off on his son Manasseh.

And Hezekiah slept with his fathers, and Manasseh his son reigned in his place. Manasseh was twelve years old when he began to reign, and he reigned fifty-five years in Jerusalem. His mother's name was Hephzibah. And he did what was evil in the sight of the Lord, according to the despicable practices of the nations whom the Lord drove out before the people of Israel. For he rebuilt the high places that Hezekiah his father had destroyed, and he erected altars for Baal and made an Asherah, as Ahab king of Israel had done, and worshipped all the host of heaven and served them.

And he built altars in the house of the Lord, of which the Lord had said, "In Jerusalem will I put my name." And he built altars for all the host of heaven in the two courts of the house of the Lord. And he burned his son as an offering and used fortune-telling and omens and dealt with mediums and with necromancers. He did much evil in the sight of the Lord, provoking him to anger (2 Kings 20:21 to 21:26 ESV).

Manasseh's son Amon follows in his father's footsteps, but Amon's son Josiah reverses the evil of his father and grandfather, and restores much of the worship to God. (2 Kings 22:1 to 23:30.)

Hezekiah was right in his wishful thinking that the destruction would not happen in his lifetime. It takes a hundred years for the whole of Judah to fall to the Babylonian army, culminating in the destruction of Jerusalem and the Temple in 586 BC (2 Kings 25:1-30), 136 years after the destruction of Samaria and Israel in the north. The people, apart from the very poor, are taken into exile in Babylon.

I have deliberately homed in on the story of Hezekiah. This should give a better idea of the problems in Israel and Judah in a snapshot of history, rather than giving the whole list of kings and their dates. There are nineteen recorded kings of Judah, plus one queen, after Solomon (c925-586 BC); and nineteen kings of Israel (c925-721 BC).

To dig deeper than this needs a larger book, and there are plenty of those available. The recorded accounts of the kings and prophets are intertwined in the Old Testament, even though their books in the Bible are not in chronological order. One way to knit them together is to find a reading plan that puts the Bible events in (probable) date order. A link to one such plan is at the start of this book, along with other recommended reading.

Chapter 8

Kingdoms come and kingdoms go. And so it is with Assyria and Babylon. All through their captivity in Babylon, the people from Judah have been talking and singing about Jerusalem. Babylon eventually falls to the Persians in 539 BC. After 70 years in captivity, the people (mostly the children and grandchildren of the original captives) are allowed home, and given permission to rebuild the Temple in Jerusalem under the supervision of Nehemiah, with Ezra as the priest. The books of Nehemiah and Ezra cover this time, with Zechariah, Haggai and Malachi the prophets. So the red cord isn't broken after all, although at one stage it looked as though it had become badly frayed. (Ezra 1:1-4.)

In the first year of Cyrus king of Persia, that the word of the Lord by the mouth of Jeremiah might be fulfilled, the Lord stirred up the spirit of Cyrus king of Persia, so that he made a proclamation throughout all his kingdom and also put it in writing: 'Thus says Cyrus king of Persia: The Lord, the God of heaven, has given me all the kingdoms of the earth, and he has charged me to build him a house at Jerusalem, which is in Judah. Whoever is among you of all his people, may his God be with him, and let him go up to Jerusalem, which is in Judah, and rebuild the house of the Lord, the God of Israel — he is the God who is in Jerusalem. And let each survivor, in whatever place he sojourns, be assisted by the men of his place with silver and gold, with goods and with beasts, besides freewill offerings for the house of God that is in Jerusalem' (Ezra 1:1-4 ESV).

This is much to the dismay and hostility of the locals who have taken over the land. Nehemiah initially concentrates on restoring the protective wall around Jerusalem and joins Ezra in leading a religious revival.

When Sanballat the Horonite and Tobiah the Ammonite servant heard this, it displeased them greatly that someone had come to seek the welfare of the people of Israel. So I went to Jerusalem and was there three days. Then I arose in the night, I and a few men with me. And I told no one what my God had put into my heart to do for Jerusalem.

There was no animal with me but the one on which I rode. I went out by night by the Valley Gate to the Dragon Spring and to the Dung Gate, and I inspected the walls of Jerusalem that were broken down and its gates that had been destroyed by fire... .

Then I said to them, "You see the trouble we are in, how Jerusalem lies in ruins with its gates burned. Come, let us build the wall of Jerusalem, that we may no longer suffer derision." And I told them of the hand of my God that had been upon me for good, and also of the words that the king had spoken to me. And they said, "Let us rise up and build"(Nehemiah 2:10-20 ESV).

The walls are eventually rebuilt and the Israelites start to live in peace. At the end of the book of the prophet Malachi in the Old Testament, the people of Judah are back in their own country, although under the authority of Persia and the Medo-Persian Empire. In Jerusalem, the Temple has been rebuilt, but it is much smaller than the one Solomon built. However, the people are united and waiting for the prophesied leader, the Messiah, to come to their aid.

Four hundred years pass before we come to the New Testament, and the only records of these years come from sources outside the Bible.

The Greeks had a great influence over that part of the world, and Alexander the Great conquers the country, now called Judea, but is persuaded not to destroy Jerusalem on his way south to invade Egypt in 332 BC.

Subsequently, a revolt led by Judas Maccabeus results in the Hasmonean dynasty of kings who ruled in Judea for over a hundred years. But in the first century BC, Rome will eventually take power, although *koine* Greek (common Greek) has became the standard language, and is the language of the New Testament writers. In 63 BC the Roman general Pompey attacks Jerusalem, and the whole country comes under the authority of Rome.

The Jews resent the Roman occupation, and are waiting for the Messiah who they now believe will form an army to deliver them from Rome. There are troubles from small groups of Jewish freedom fighters.

Pompey and the Roman Senate appoint Herod Antipater (Antipas) as the Procurator of Judea, and make his two sons kings of Judea in the south, and Galilee in the north. The son who becomes king of Judea is Herod the Great. To appease the Jews, Herod builds them a new Temple. He is, however, disturbed by news from visitors from the east, who tell him that a new king has been born. Actually, he is terrified. Some Jews are causing him enough trouble as it is. Surely there is not to be a rival!

Now after Jesus was born in Bethlehem of Judea in the days of Herod the king, behold, wise men from the east came to Jerusalem, saying, "Where is he who has been born king of the Jews? For we saw his star when it rose and have come to worship him." When Herod the king heard this, he was troubled, and all Jerusalem with him (Matthew 2:1-3 ESV).

Chapter 9

For to us a child is born, to us a son is given; and the government shall be upon his shoulder, and his name shall be called Wonderful Counsellor, Mighty God, Everlasting Father, Prince of Peace (Isaiah 9:6 9 ESV).

This verse is not from the New Testament. It was written by Isaiah 700 years before the birth of Jesus, and is one of several prophesying the birth and death of Jesus. The Jews have been waiting for this child for centuries. The time has finally come.

In the sixth month the angel Gabriel was sent from God to a town in Galilee called Nazareth, to a virgin betrothed to a man whose name was Joseph, of the house of David. And the virgin's name was Mary. And he came to her and said, "Greetings, O favoured one, the Lord is with you!"

But she was greatly troubled at the saying, and tried to discern what sort of greeting this might be.

And the angel said to her, "Do not be afraid, Mary, for you have found favour with God. And behold, you will conceive in your womb and bear a son, and you shall call his name Jesus. He will be great and will be called the Son of the Most High. And the Lord God will give to him the throne of his father David, and he will reign over the house of Jacob forever, and of his kingdom there will be no end."

And Mary said to the angel, "How will this be, since I am a virgin?"

And the angel answered her, "The Holy Spirit will come upon you, and the power of the Most High will overshadow you; therefore the child to be born will be called holy — the Son of God (Luke 1 ESV).

John, an eyewitness, writes in one of his letters: And we have seen and testify that the Father has sent his Son to be the Saviour of the world (1 John 4:14 ESV). I cannot possibly summarise the life of Jesus in a couple of pages. I suggest you read one of the four Gospels, perhaps Mark for starters. Jesus grows up, and when he is about thirty years old he begins his ministry in his hometown, Nazareth.

Jesus returned in the power of the Spirit to Galilee, and a report about him went out through all the surrounding country. And he taught in their synagogues, being glorified by all.

And he came to Nazareth, where he had been brought up. And as was his custom, he went to the synagogue on the Sabbath day (our Saturday), and he stood up to read. And the scroll of the prophet Isaiah was given to him.

He unrolled the scroll and found the place where it was written, "The Spirit of the Lord is upon me, because he has anointed me to proclaim good news to the poor. He has sent me to proclaim liberty to the captives and recovering of sight to the blind, to set at liberty those who are oppressed, to proclaim the year of the Lord's favour."

And he rolled up the scroll and gave it back to the attendant and sat down. And the eyes of all in the synagogue were fixed on him. And he began to say to them, "Today this Scripture has been fulfilled in your hearing." And all spoke well of him and marvelled at the gracious words that were coming from his mouth. And they said, "Is not this Joseph's son?" (Luke 1 ESV).

As soon as Jesus points out that the Scriptures foretell his coming, this doesn't go down well when they realize he isn't a "famous" preacher from outside, but that he grew up in Nazareth.

When they heard these things, all in the synagogue were filled with wrath. And they rose up and drove him out of the town and brought him to the brow of the hill on which their town was built, so that they could throw him down the cliff. But passing through their midst, he went away.

Jesus is recorded in the Gospels as doing many miracles, teaching his Sermon of the Mount, and claiming to be the Messiah and the Son of God. He has many followers, and selects twelve to be his main disciples. There are three chapters in Matthew on the Sermon on the Mount. (Matthew 5:1 to 7:27.) You must read them for yourself. In the Gospels you can see how the red cord binds God's plan for rescue, in the life, death and resurrection of Jesus.

Eventually Jesus has upset the Jewish authorities too much, and they plan to kill him. This comes as no surprise to Jesus, for he says he came to die, to be a sacrifice for forgiveness of sins — our sins.

"The Son of Man did not come to be served, but to serve, and to give his life as a ransom for many" (Matthew 20:28 ESV).

And so the plan comes into action. Jesus is arrested and tried before the governor Pilate. Pilate finds Jesus not guilty, but the Jewish leaders scream for him to be executed. Fearing a riot, Pilate hands Jesus over for crucifixion — the cruellest form of execution the Romans can devise.

So when Pilate saw that he was gaining nothing, but rather that a riot was beginning, he took water and washed his hands before the crowd, saying, "I am innocent of this man's blood; see to it yourselves." And all the people answered, "His blood be on us and on our children!" ...

Then the soldiers of the governor took Jesus into the governor's headquarters, and they gathered the whole battalion before him. And they stripped him and put a red robe on him, and twisting together a crown of thorns, they put it on his head and put a reed in his right hand. And kneeling before him, they mocked him, saying, "Hail, King of the Jews!" ...

And when they came to a place called Golgotha (which means Place of a Skull), they offered him wine to drink, mixed with gall, but when he tasted it, he would not drink it. And when they had crucified him, they divided his garments among them by casting lots... .

The scribes and elders, mocked him, saying, "He saved others; he cannot save himself. He is the King of Israel; let him come down now from the cross, and we will believe in him. He trusts in God; let God deliver him now, if he desires him. For he said, 'I am the Son of God.'" ...

Now from the sixth hour there was darkness over all the land until the ninth hour... . And Jesus cried out again with a loud voice and yielded up his spirit. And behold, the curtain of the Temple was torn in two, from top to bottom. And the earth shook, and the rocks were split... . When the centurion and those who were with him, keeping watch over Jesus, saw the earthquake and what took place, they were filled with awe and said, "Truly this was the Son of God!" There were also many women there, looking on from a distance, who had followed Jesus from Galilee, ministering to him, among whom were Mary Magdalene and Mary the mother of James and Joseph and the mother of the sons of Zebedee (Matthew 27:24-62 ESV).

Joseph from Arimathea persuades Pilate to allow him to take the body of Jesus for burial in his own, previously unused, tomb.

The next day, that is, after the day of Preparation, the chief priests and the Pharisees gathered before Pilate and said, "Sir, we remember how that impostor said, while he was still alive, 'After three days I will rise.' Therefore order the tomb to be made secure until the third day, lest his disciples go and steal him away and tell the people, 'He has risen from the dead,' and the last fraud will be worse than the first." Pilate said to them, "You have a guard of soldiers. Go, make it as secure as you can."

Chapter 10

Guards and a heavy stone cannot seal the Son of God in a tomb. On the third day the tomb is empty. As he promised, Jesus has risen from the dead, on the first day of the week — the day we now call Sunday. Luke gives us more details in his Gospel.

The women who had come with him from Galilee followed and saw the tomb and how his body was laid. Then they returned and prepared spices and ointments. On the Sabbath they rested according to the commandment. But on the first day of the week, at early dawn, they went to the tomb, taking the spices they had prepared. And they found the stone rolled away from the tomb, but when they went in they did not find the body of the Lord Jesus. While they were perplexed about this, behold, two men stood by them in dazzling apparel.

... The men said to them, "Why do you seek the living among the dead? He is not here, but has risen. Remember how he told you, while he was still in Galilee, that the Son of Man must be delivered into the hands of sinful men and be crucified and on the third day rise."

And they remembered his words, and returning from the tomb they told all these things to the eleven and to all the rest. Now it was Mary Magdalene and Joanna and Mary the mother of James and the other women with them who told these things to the apostles, but these words seemed to them an idle tale, and they did not believe them.

But Peter rose and ran to the tomb; stooping and looking in, he saw the linen cloths by themselves; and he went home marvelling at what had happened....

As they were talking about these things, Jesus himself stood among them, and said to them, "Peace to you!"

But they were startled and frightened and thought they saw a spirit. And he said to them, "Why are you troubled, and why do doubts arise in your hearts? See my hands and my feet, that it is I myself. Touch me, and see. For a spirit does not have flesh and bones as you see that I have." And when he had said this, he showed them his hands and his feet... .

Then he opened their minds to understand the Scriptures, and said to them, "Thus it is written, that the Christ should suffer and on the third day rise from the dead, and that repentance and forgiveness of sins should be proclaimed in his name to all nations, beginning from Jerusalem. You are witnesses of these things."

He led them out as far as Bethany, and lifting up his hands he blessed them. While he blessed them, he parted from them and was carried up into heaven. And they worshipped him and returned to Jerusalem with great joy, and were continually in the Temple blessing God (Luke 23:50 to 24:53 ESV).

Jesus is with his disciples and other friends for forty days before returning to heaven. The apostle Paul writes that more than five hundred people saw the risen Jesus on a single occasion, most of whom were still alive at the time he wrote about it.

For I delivered to you as of first importance what I also received: that Christ died for our sins in accordance with the Scriptures, that he was buried, that he was raised on the third day in accordance with the Scriptures, and that he appeared to Cephas [Peter], then to the twelve. Then he appeared to more than five hundred brothers at one time, most of whom are still alive, though some have fallen asleep. Then he appeared to James, then to all the apostles. Last of all, as to one untimely born, he appeared also to me. For I am the least of the apostles, unworthy to be called an apostle, because I persecuted the church of God (1 Corinthians 15:3-9 ESV).

And this leads us on to the early Christian church where Paul, a strict Jewish Pharisee called Saul at the time, will shortly set out to eliminate all Christians. But he will be reckoning without the power of the Holy Spirit who is coming down on the disciples where they are meeting together.

When the day of Pentecost arrived, they were all together in one place. And suddenly there came from heaven a sound like a mighty rushing wind, and it filled the entire house where they were sitting. And divided tongues as of fire appeared to them and rested on each one of them.

And they were all filled with the Holy Spirit and began to speak in other tongues as the Spirit gave them utterance.... . And all were amazed and perplexed, saying to one another, "What does this mean?" But others mocking said, "They are filled with new wine."

But Peter, standing with the eleven, lifted up his voice and addressed them: "Men of Judea and all who dwell in Jerusalem, let this be known to you, and give ear to my words. For these people are not drunk, as you suppose, since it is only the third hour of the day. But this is what was uttered through the prophet Joel: "'And in the last days it shall be, God declares, that I will pour out my Spirit on all flesh, and your sons and your daughters shall prophesy, and your young men shall see visions, and your old men shall dream dreams; even on my male servants and female servants in those days I will pour out my Spirit, and they shall prophesy. And I will show wonders in the heavens above and signs on the earth below, blood, and fire, and vapour of smoke; the sun shall be turned to darkness and the moon to blood, before the day of the Lord comes, the great and magnificent day. And it shall come to pass that everyone who calls upon the name of the Lord shall be saved.'

"Men of Israel, hear these words: Jesus of Nazareth, a man attested to you by God with mighty works and wonders and signs that God did through him in your midst, as you yourselves know — this Jesus, delivered up according to the definite plan and foreknowledge of God, you crucified and killed by the hands of lawless men. God raised him up, loosing the pangs of death, because it was not possible for him to be held by it" (Acts 2:1-24 ESV).

Stephen is the first recorded Christian martyr, and Paul is present at his stoning outside the walls at Jerusalem, cheering the crowd on, and keeping watch on the coats of the killers.

Stephen, full of grace and power, was doing great wonders and signs among the people. Then some ... could not withstand the wisdom and the Spirit with which he was speaking (Acts 6:8 to 7:60 ESV).

Stephen tells the listeners about Jesus, but what he has to say makes some of the Jewish leaders angry. They do not want to hear that they have crucified the Son of God.

Now when they heard these things they were enraged, and they ground their teeth at him. But he, full of the Holy Spirit, gazed into heaven and saw the glory of God, and Jesus standing at the right hand of God. And he said, "Behold, I see the heavens opened, and the Son of Man standing at the right hand of God." But they cried out with a loud voice and stopped their ears and rushed together at him. Then they cast him out of the city and stoned him. And the witnesses laid down their garments at the feet of a young man called Saul. And as they were stoning Stephen, he called out, "Lord Jesus, receive my spirit." And falling to his knees he cried out with a loud voice, "Lord, do not hold this sin against them." And when he had said this, he fell asleep.

This is just the start of the persecution of Christians, something that is still happening in many countries today, where Christian are literally losing their lives for their faith. But the red cord of rescue is holding fast.

But Saul, still breathing threats and murder against the disciples of the Lord, went to the high priest and asked him for letters to the synagogues at Damascus, so that if he found any belonging to the Way, men or women, he might bring them bound to Jerusalem... . He approached Damascus, and suddenly a light from heaven flashed around him. And falling to the ground he heard a voice saying to him, "Saul, Saul, why are you persecuting me?" And he said, "Who are you, Lord?" And he said, "I am Jesus, whom you are persecuting. But rise and enter the city, and you will be told what you are to do" (Acts 9:1-31 ESV). See also Acts 22:1-21 and Acts 26:1-23.

Saul gets his new name of Paul, and his life is changed completely by this encounter with Jesus. He becomes one of the greatest Christian preachers and writers, travelling on missionary journeys, with others, to start churches all around the Mediterranean, and often returning to make sure they are growing in the faith. He also writes letters to these new churches, encouraging them — and even admonishing them when he hears disturbing news about some of the church members. We can read some of these letters (also known as epistles) in the New Testament today, along with some short(ish) letters from the apostles James, Peter, John and Jude.

The final book, Revelation, is a mix of warnings from God to seven churches that are not all they should be, with prophecies, visions, and promises for the future. This is probably the best known promise, where the other end of our red cord is anchored:

"Behold, the dwelling place of God is with man. He will dwell with them, and they will be his people, and God himself will be with them as their God. He will wipe away every tear from their eyes, and death shall be no more, neither shall there be mourning, nor crying, nor pain anymore, for the former things have passed away" (Revelation 21:1-4 ESV).

The Finishing Post

We have managed to reach the finishing post and the red cord is still tied firmly to that reassuring news in Revelation at the end of our last chapter. God's plan for us came good with the birth, death and resurrection of Jesus. We have been bought with a price — the blood of Jesus.

I have already included part of the book of Acts. In it, you can read how the first missionaries, filled with the Holy Spirit, set out to tell the good news of Jesus to the towns and cities around the Mediterranean. Life was hard and dangerous, and many of the apostles and others gave their lives for what they knew to be true. Here, Paul is leaving the members of the Ephesian church for the last time.

I know that after my departure fierce wolves will come in among you, not sparing the flock; and from among your own selves will arise men speaking twisted things, to draw away the disciples after them. Therefore be alert, remembering that for three years I did not cease night or day to admonish everyone with tears. And now I commend you to God and to the word of his grace, which is able to build you up and to give you the inheritance among all those who are sanctified (Acts 20:17-38 ESV).

Paul and others are kept busy, visiting and writing letters to the new Christian churches. Some churches consist of Jewish converts where members, who want to continue the established Jewish traditions, try to force Gentile (non-Jewish) converts to adopt their practices.

Other churches are made up of gentile converts, where members are keeping a foot in the camp of their old religion. Others somehow get it right. It is to this mix of churches that the rest of the New Testament letters are written — and they are essential reading for Christians today. The teaching in the letters is powerful, and some of the most memorable promises in the Bible are in there. Be sure to read them.

Paul wrote the first series of letters in the New Testament, followed by the writing of other apostles, with the book of Revelation at the very end.

The book of Hebrews, near the middle of the New Testament letters, was written to Jewish converts to show them that Jesus was foretold in the Scriptures (our Old Testament — which is where our run through the Bible began) making it clear that the blood of animal sacrifices has been replaced once and for all by the blood of Jesus on the Cross — our red cord.

I am aware that I have had to leave out many, many important people, places and events, but to put them in 42 small pages (of the paperback edition) would have resulted in a book consisting of little more than a long list, with sparse details. I want to show that the Bible is not a dusty old book that's difficult to understand. It's exciting and challenging, and very relevant for us today. Now, hopefully, when you read or hear about these missing names and events, you will be able to picture them in their correct timescale and location — while keeping an eye out for the red cord of God's salvation plan.

God speaks to us through the Bible. This quote from the apostle Paul, in a letter to his missionary friend Timothy, makes a memorable and powerful ending to this book:

All Scripture is breathed out by God and profitable for teaching, for reproof, for correction, and for training in righteousness (2 Timothy 3:16 ESV).

THE END

White Tree Publishing

White Tree Publishing publishes mainstream evangelical Christian literature in paperback and eBook formats, for people of all ages. We aim to make our eBooks available free for all eBook devices, but some distributors will only list our books free at their discretion, and may make a small charge for some titles — but they are still great value!

More Bible-related books from White Tree Publishing are on the next pages, some of which are available as both eBooks and paperbacks. Many more Christian books than those shown here are available in non-fiction, fiction, and titles for younger readers. The full list of published and forthcoming books is on our website www.whitetreepublishing.com. Please visit there regularly for updates.

We rely on our readers to tell their families, friends and churches about our books. Social media is a great way of doing this. Take a look at our range of fiction and non-fiction books and pass the word on. You can even contact your favourite Christian TV or radio programme to let them know about these books. Also, please write a positive review on the distributor's site if you are able.

eBook edition of this book is available
in all formats

eBook ISBN: 978-0-9935005-9-6

Four short books of help in the Christian life:

So, What Is a Christian? An introduction to a personal faith. Paperback ISBN: 978-0-9927642-2-7, eBook ISBN: 978-0-9933941-2-6

Starting Out — help for new Christians of all ages. Paperback ISBN 978-1-4839-622-0-7, eBook ISBN: 978-0-9933941-0-2

Help! — Explores some problems we can encounter with our faith. Paperback ISBN 978-0-9927642-2-7, eBook ISBN: 978-0-9933941-1-9

Running Through the Bible — a simple understanding of what's in the Bible — Paperback ISBN: 978-0-9927642-6-5, eBook ISBN: 978-0-9933941-3-3

Blunt's Scriptural Coincidences
Gospels and Acts
J. J. Blunt
New Edition

This book will confirm (or restore) your faith in the Gospel records. Clearly the Gospels were not invented. There is too much unintentional agreement between them for this to be so. Undesigned coincidences are where writers tell the same account, but from a different viewpoint. Without conspiring together to get their accounts in agreement, they include unexpected (and often unnoticed) details that corroborate their records. Not only are these unexpected coincidences found within the Gospels, but sometimes a historical writer unknowingly and unintentionally confirms the Bible record.

Within these pages you will see just how accurate were the memories of the Gospel writers — even of the smallest details which on casual reading can seem of little importance, yet clearly point to eyewitness accounts. J.J. Blunt spent many years investigating these coincidences. And here they are, as found in the four Gospels and Acts.

First published in instalments between 1833 and 1847
The edition used here published in 1876

eBook only
ISBN: 978-0-9935005-5-8

Be Still
Bible Words of Peace and Comfort

There may come a time in our lives when we want to concentrate on God's many promises of peace and comfort. The Bible readings in this book are for people who need to know what it means to be held securely in the Lord's loving arms.

Rather than selecting single verses here and there, each reading in this book is a run of several verses. This gives a much better picture of the whole passage in which a favourite verse may be found.

As well as being for personal use, these readings are

intended for sharing with anyone in special need, to help them draw comfort from the reading and prayer for that date. Bible reading and prayer are the two most important ways of getting to know and trust Jesus Christ, our Lord and Saviour.

The reference to the verses for the day are given, for you to look up and read in your preferred Bible translation.

eBook ISBN: 978-0-9933941-4-0

Paperback ISBN: 978-0-9932760-7-1
116 pages   5x7.8 inches

A Previously Unpublished Book
The Simplicity of the Incarnation
J Stafford Wright
Foreword by J I Packer

"I believe in … Jesus Christ … born of the Virgin Mary." A beautiful stained glass image, or a medical reality? This is the choice facing Christians today. Can we truly believe that two thousand years ago a young woman, a virgin named Mary, gave birth to the Son of God? The answer is simple: we can.

The author says, *"In these days many Christians want some sensible assurance that their faith makes sense, and in this book I want to show that it does."*

274

In this uplifting book from a previously unpublished and recently discovered manuscript, J Stafford Wright investigates the reality of the incarnation, looks at the crucifixion and resurrection of Jesus, and helps the reader understand more of the Trinity and the certainty of eternal life in heaven.

This book was written shortly before the author's death in 1985. *The Simplicity of the Incarnation* is published for the first time, unedited, from his final draft.

eBook ISBN 13: 978-0-9932760-5-7

Paperback ISBN: 9-780-9525-9563-2
160 pages 5.25 x 8 inches
Available from bookstores and major internet sellers

Bible People Real People
An Unforgettable A-Z of Who is Who in the Bible

In a fascinating look at real people, J Stafford Wright shows his love and scholarly knowledge of the Bible as he brings the characters from its pages to life in a memorable way.
Read this book through from A to Z, like any other title
Dip in and discover who was who in personal Bible study
Check the names when preparing a talk or sermon

The good, the bad, the beautiful and the ugly – no one is spared. This is a book for everyone who wants to get to grips with the reality that is in the pages of the Bible, the Word of God.

With the names arranged in alphabetical order, the Old and New Testament characters are clearly identified so that the reader is able to explore either the Old or New Testament people on the first reading, and the other Testament on the second.

Those wanting to become more familiar with the Bible will find this is a great introduction to the people inhabiting the best selling book in the world, and those who can quote chapter and verse will find everyone suddenly becomes much more real – because these people *are* real. This is a book to keep handy and refer to frequently while reading the Bible.

"For students of my generation the name Stafford Wright was associated with the spiritual giants of his generation. Scholarship and integrity were the hallmarks of his biblical teaching. He taught us the faith and inspired our discipleship of Christ. To God be the Glory." The Rt. Rev. James Jones, Bishop of Liverpool

This is a lively, well-informed study of some great Bible characters. Professor Gordon Wenham MA PhD. Tutor in Old Testament at Trinity College Bristol and Emeritus Professor of Old Testament at the University of Gloucestershire.

eBook ISBN: 978-0-9932760-7-1

Paperback ISBN: 978-0-9525956-5-6
314 pages 6x9 inches
Note: This book is not available in all eBook formats

English Hexapla
The Gospel of John
(Paperback only)

Published to coincide with the 400th anniversary of the Authorized King James Version of the Bible, this book contains the full text of Bagster's assembled work for the Gospel of John. On each page in parallel columns are the words of the six most important translations of the New Testament into English, made between 1380 and 1611. Below the English is the original Greek text after Scholz.

To enhance the reading experience, there is an introduction telling how we got our English Bibles, with significant pages from early Bibles shown at the end of the book.

Here is an opportunity to read English that once split the Church by giving ordinary people the power to discover God's word for themselves. Now you can step back in time and discover those words and spellings for yourself, as they first appeared hundreds of years ago.

Wyclif 1380, Tyndale 1534, Cranmer 1539, Geneva 1557, Douay Rheims 1582, Authorized (KJV) 1611.

English Hexapla — The Gospel of John
Published by White Tree Publishing

Available in paperback only.
Paperback ISBN: 978-0-9525956-1-8
Size 7.5 x 9.7 inches paperback
Not available as an eBook

eBook due March 2017

The Authority and Interpretation of the Bible

J Stafford Wright

When we start to think about God, we soon come to a point where we say, "I can discover nothing more about God by myself. I must see whether He has revealed anything about Himself, about His character, and about the way to find Him and to please Him." From the beginning, the Christian church has believed that certain writings were the Word of God in a unique sense. Before the New Testament was compiled, Christians accepted the Old Testament as their sacred Book. Here they were following the example of Christ Himself. During His ministry Jesus Christ made great use of the Old Testament, and after His resurrection He spent some time in teaching His disciples that every section of the Old Testament had teachings in it concerning Himself. Any discussion of the inspiration of the Bible gives place sooner or later to a discussion of its interpretation. To say that the Bible is true, or infallible, is not sufficient: for it is one thing to have an infallible Book, and quite another to use it. **J Stafford Wright** was a greatly respected evangelical theologian and author, and former Principal of Tyndale Hall Theological College, Bristol.

eBook only
eBook ISBN: 978-0-9954549-9-6